INFORMATION FOR THOSE WHO HAVE ONLY MINUTES TO READ

THE
BIBLE
BATHROOM
BOOK

HOWARD BOOKS
A Division of Simon & Schuster
New York   London   Toronto   Sydney

MARK LITTLETON

Our purpose at Howard Books is to:
- *Increase faith* in the hearts of growing Christians
- *Inspire holiness* in the lives of believers
- *Instill hope* in the hearts of struggling people everywhere

Because He's coming again!

 Published by Howard Books, a division of Simon & Schuster, Inc.
1230 Avenue of the Americas, New York, NY 10020
www.howardpublishing.com

Library of Congress Cataloging-in-Publication Data
Littleton, Mark R.
  The Bible bathroom book : information for those who have only minutes to read / Mark Littleton.
    p. cm.
  Summary: "A collection of information, trivia, definitions, quotes, and lists about the Bible in a format for quick, easy reading"—Provided by publisher.
  1. Bible—Miscellanea. I. Title.
  BS538.L58 2008
  220—dc 22
                              2007032435
ISBN-13: 978-1-4165-4359-6
ISBN-10:   1-4165-4359-7

10 9 8 7 6 5 4 3 2 1

Manufactured in the United States of America

For information regarding special discounts for bulk purchases, please contact: Simon & Schuster Special Sales at 1-800-456-6798 or business@simonandschuster.com.

Edited by Mary McNeil
Cover design by Greg Jackson, Thinkpen Design, Inc.
Interior design by John Mark Luke Designs

To my daughter *Alisha,*

who at the age of seventeen committed her life to Jesus in a way that marvelously changed her forever, in a multitude of wonderful ways that maybe someday I will write about. I look forward to seeing you grow in the likeness of Jesus in the days ahead. And if you read this book and it helps, let me know. I'd be interested to hear of anything new you learned or any points you happen to disagree with.

CONTENTS

CONTENTS

BEYOND BASIC BIBLE

CONTENTS

BIT O' BIBLE

DIG IT UP

CONTENTS

FANTASTIC OR FAKE?

FAST FACTS

CONTENTS

CONTENTS

CONTENTS

CONTENTS

CONTENTS

CONTENTS

MOVERS AND SHAKERS OF THE BIBLE

CONTENTS

SPEAKING OF THE BIBLE

STRANGE BUT TRUE

CONTENTS

CONTENTS

TOUGH QUESTIONS

ACKNOWLEDGMENTS

Thanks to a number of people who have helped in the production of this book:

Dr. John MacArthur, editor of *The MacArthur Study Bible* and Dr. Charles Ryrie, editor of *The Ryrie Study Bible*, whose notes in those texts were very helpful to me.

Josh McDowell, for the great factual information about archaeology in *Evidence That Demands a Verdict*.

To the authors of many other books I used in the process of writing this book who must go unnamed because there are simply too many of them. God knows who you are, though, and one day you will learn of your contributions here as well as in a multitude of other ways.

Also, thanks to Dan Brown, author of *The Da Vinci Code*, whose book, so full of misinformation, myths, and fakery, made me want to write something to tell some of the real truth about my favorite book, the Bible.

To Denny Boultinghouse, John and Chrys Howard, and the editors and staff at Howard Books who have made this book possible and who gave me the opportunity to write it. Also, to Mary McNeil, freelance editor extraordinaire, who pulled this book together in a way I never could have anticipated.

To my wife, Jeanette, and kids, Alisha, Gardner, and Elizabeth, who didn't stop me too often to ask questions like "Will you change my diaper?" (Elizabeth), "Look at these worms I found in the backyard, Dad" (Gardner), and "I need a check for two hundred forty dollars for Summerfest, Dad, so will you please write it out? Now" (Alisha). Oh, and, "Come to bed, honey; I'm lonely" (Jeanette).

Most of all, thanks to God the Father, the Son, and the Holy Spirit. They're the ones who really made all this possible. If not for them, I'd probably be high somewhere, writing poems about weird thoughts in my head, and wondering where I would go when I died. Fortunately, they have told me where I'm going. I stopped the drug bit years ago. Today I'm writing books like this.

However, I still do write poems now and then out of the weird thoughts that still course through my head. (Maybe that will be my next book: "Weird thoughts in my head.") Do you think I can convince Howard Books to do that one too?

HOW to USE
THIS BOOK

This is a book about the Bible, but it is not a Bible dictionary, encyclopedia, or reference book. Yes, the facts are facts (and any fictions are made obvious). But they are arranged in a way to make quick, easy reading, such as you might do while sitting on the toilet or after taking a shower. It does not demean the Bible at all that I have conceived of this book as a "bathroom" book. Everyone reads something while using the bathroom; it's a good way to pass the time (no pun intended). Why not, then, read something with substance, but not so much substance that your mind starts to quiver, moan, and wail with the intensity of a person undergoing "flaming death" à la *A Bug's Life*? (If you haven't seen it, ask your children; they'll know all about it.)

This book gives you bite-size chunks of information that are fun, interesting, engrossing, compelling, and at times humorous, gross, and/or idiotic. I admit, some of the fun in this book comes strictly from my own sense of humor, which has been described as "moronic" by my wife, "subhuman" by my eighteen-year-old daughter in college, and "really cool" by my nine-year-old. Alas, there are no booger jokes for those of you who pick these out immediately (another pun not intended). I'd just like you to have some fun, learn some truths about the Bible, and pass the time without straining yourself.

Once you're done reading a selection, you can put the book down until the next occasion. But you will have learned something in the process, perhaps something useful and good.

The book is not organized around any central principle (other than the Bible, of course). It's a mishmash of data, jumping from the Old Testament to the New Testament and back again. You will find lists of various kinds, Q & A's, info dumps, weird facts and truths, and everything else you can imagine.

It's my hope that you will learn much in this book about the Bible that you didn't know before. Ultimately, my greatest joy would be to learn that this data has changed your life for the better in some way.

BIBLE TRIVIA

How good is your knowledge of Bible trivia?

1. How many different books are in the Old Testament?

2. How many books are in the New Testament?

3. How many different people wrote books of the Bible?

4. What languages was the Bible originally written in?

5. Which book of the Bible is about "beginnings"?

6. Which book of the Bible is about the future?

7. What is the longest book of the Bible?

8. What is the shortest book of the Bible?

9. What is the shortest chapter in the Bible?

10. What is the longest chapter in the Bible?

Answers:

1. 39

2. 27

3. 40

4. Hebrew, Aramaic, and Koine (common) Greek

5. Genesis

6. Revelation

7. Psalms

8. 2 John

9. Psalm 117

10. Psalm 119

WHAT'S IN THE BIBLE?

The Bible is composed of sixty-six separate books or writings. There are thirty-nine specific books by various authors in the Old Testament, and twenty-seven in the New Testament. These books use many different styles of writing. For instance, the first five books of the Old Testament are known as the Torah to Jewish readers or the Books of the Law. These include laws, history, and anecdotal-type stories. Following these are the books of history, from Joshua to Esther. These contain historical details about specific people, times, situations, wars, and so on.

Following these books are the poetry books, from Job to the Song of Songs. These are called poetry not because they are poetic with rhyme and meter like we might think of poetry, but because they are Hebrew forms of poetry, which involve the use of wordplay, symbols, metaphors, similes, and so on.

After these, we have the Major Prophets (from Isaiah to Daniel) and the Minor Prophets, from Hosea to Malachi. These books are all prophetic in nature in that they either contain specific "forth-telling," which is what God does when he wants to admonish or shame his listeners, and "fore-telling" when God wants to predict some future event.

In the New Testament, you find books of history from Matthew to Acts, letters to the church from Paul and others, from Romans to Jude, and more prophecy—the book of Revelation.

Strangely enough, the Bible contains several forms of writing you probably wouldn't normally expect in a religious tome. There's drama, with different speaking parts as in Job and the Song of Songs. Throughout the Bible you find many parables, or short pithy stories designed to teach a point. You will find these mostly in the four Gospels (Matthew through John) as told by Jesus, but you can also read them in many other places throughout the Bible (such as the story used by the prophet Nathan to convict King David of his sin of adultery and murder—see 2 Samuel 12).

You will also read statements that God doesn't agree with, as in the book of Job or the antics of Satan in various places. There are sermons, as in the whole book of Deuteronomy and throughout the Gospels when Jesus preached. Events like miracles, sins (like Cain killing Abel), and proverbs will all inform us in graphic ways of what God wants us to know about himself and his acts in human history.

The Bible uniquely speaks to the youngest children and the oldest adults. In it, there is something for everyone, including you.

NEWSFLASH!

When you read the Bible, one of the best ways to approach it is simply to read the stories and reporting as if it were your daily newspaper. Don't worry about issues like "inspiration" and the fact that it's called "the Word of God." The Bible was written for common people, regular dudes and dudesses, and not for highfalutin scholars and priests alone. It's God's message to each of us, and much of it is directly on our level. This is one reason you don't find great detail in many places (like the story of Creation in Genesis 1). God wrote to speak to the average person, not someone with a PhD or master of theology after his name.

THE VERY BEST PLACE TO START

Many people want to know where to start reading when they open a Bible. In the Old Testament, the first books to read are Genesis and Exodus, then 1 and 2

Samuel, Proverbs, and Daniel. In the New Testament, it's best to start with one of the four Gospels, preferably Luke or John, then move on to Acts, one of the letters of Paul (Ephesians, Philippians, or 1 Thessalonians), and then move on to the more difficult books: Romans, 1 and 2 Corinthians, and so on. Reading about three or four chapters a day will get you through the whole Bible in one year. But don't get bogged down in Leviticus!

WHAT SOME WELL-KNOWN PEOPLE HAVE SAID ABOUT THE BEST-KNOWN BOOK

Martin Luther, the cause and founder of the Protestant Reformation in 1517, said, "The Bible is alive, it speaks to me; it has feet, it runs after me; it has hands, it lays hold on me."

Abraham Lincoln felt so strongly about its importance that he said, "I believe the Bible is the best gift that God has ever given to man. All the good from the Saviour of the world is communicated to us through this Book. All the things desirable to man are contained in it. I have been driven to my knees by the overwhelming conviction that I had nowhere else to go."

Wilbur Smith, a twentieth-century writer who plunged into the Bible's depths with vigor and faith, said, "Whatever one may think of the authority of and the message presented in the book we call the Bible, there is worldwide agreement that in more ways than one it is the most remarkable volume that has ever been produced in these some five thousand years of writing on the part of the human race."

And the great cinematographer *Cecil B. DeMille,* when once asked why he produced so many movies about the Bible, said, "Why let two thousand years of publicity go to waste!"

Robert E. Lee, general of the Confederate Army during the American Civil War: "The Bible is a book in comparison with which all others in my eyes are of minor importance, and which in all my perplexities and distresses has never failed to give me light and strength."

Immanuel Kant, German philosopher: "The Bible is an inexhaustible fountain of all truths. The existence of the Bible is the greatest blessing which humanity ever experienced."

Will H. Houghton: "Lay hold on the Bible until the Bible lays hold on you."

Victor Hugo, nineteenth-century French novelist: "England has two books: the Bible and Shakespeare. England made Shakespeare but the Bible made England."

Theodore Roosevelt, former president of the United States: "If a man is not familiar with the Bible, he has suffered a loss which he had better make all possible haste to correct."

John Herschel, Jewish astronomer: "All human discoveries seem to be made only for the purpose of confirming more and more strongly the truths contained in the Holy Scriptures."

A.W. Tozer, twentieth-century Christian author and mystic: "I did not go through the Book. The Book went through me."

ABBA

This was the personal name Jesus called his Father in heaven, according to Mark 14:36. There, Jesus addressed God as "Abba" in the Garden of Gethsemane, where he begged to be released from being crucified. He said, "Abba, Father, everything is possible for you. Take this cup from me. Yet not what I will, but what you will." God did not let Jesus off, though, and Jesus went to the cross willingly, even though in the process of praying, he sweat "drops of blood" because of the horror he felt in facing the event.

Later in the New Testament, Paul offered the same term for Christians to use, representing intimacy and familiarity to the Father. "Abba" is the Middle Eastern term for "Papa," or "Daddy." Paul mentioned it in the following passages:

ROMANS 8:15–16: *"You did not receive a spirit that makes you a slave again to fear, but you received the Spirit of sonship. And by him we cry, 'Abba, Father.' The Spirit himself testifies with our spirit that we are God's children."*

GALATIANS 4:6: *"Because you are sons, God sent the Spirit of his Son into our hearts, the Spirit who calls out, 'Abba, Father.'"*

THE YEAR OF THE LORD

A.D. comes from the Latin anno Domini ("the year of the Lord"), meaning the years that follow the birth of Christ. Before A.D. was B.C. ("before Christ"), which some have tried to change to B.C.E. ("before the Christian era") a bit unsuccessfully. The dating was originally based on calculations done by Dionysius Exiguus in A.D. 527. He thought Jesus was born in A.D. 0, though later discoveries have proved him wrong. However, the dating system still remains. It's one reason some people have said that "history" is "His story"—Jesus's story and work in the world.

The system of A.D. and B.C. anchor the Gregorian calendar, designed and put into effect by Pope Gregory XIII in 1582.

REBORN?

The phrase *born again* is used in many ways in the United States and around the world. Sports writers said that Michael Jordan's basketball career was "born again" after he left the NBA to play professional baseball, failed at it, and returned to the NBA to become its greatest star. Entertainers suggested Madonna has been "born again" several times as she "reinvents" herself to her audience in various ways.

The first person to use the term was Jesus. You'll find it in John 3:3, where Jesus speaks at night with a Pharisee and teacher named Nicodemus. This seeker wanted to know the truth but sought Jesus at night so he could do this in private and avoid the fallout from his fellow Pharisees about consorting with the hated "pretender" Jesus. Though he would later become a believer, at this point he is a seeker and probably honestly trying to come to grips with what Jesus taught. Jesus said to Nicodemus, after the Pharisee said he knew Jesus was a teacher from God, "I tell you the truth, no one can see the kingdom of God unless he is born again." Jesus repeated the words in John 3:7. The idea is also found one more time in 1 Peter 1:23. You will find the phrase "new birth" also in 1 Peter 1:3.

What was Jesus's meaning? He clarified it in John 3:5, when he said a person must be "born of water and the Spirit." This phrasing has received a lot of controversy and discussion for two millennia, but it appears that Jesus meant the process of salvation. He was saying a person has to undergo a complete transformation that was like starting over as a new person, the same way a birth begins a person's life. Paul said when this happens, the Christian is a "new creation" (2 Corinthians 5:17). Thus, when we're born again, God opens our eyes in a spiritual way and we see the kingdom of God in a way physical eyes cannot. Being born again is a divine spiritual experience. All who trust Jesus as Savior and Lord enter a special relationship with God too. They are born into God's family through being "born again," and they discover the reality of God's presence and person in a special, divine way.

WHAT IS A CHRISTIAN?

How do you tell if a person is really a "Christian"? In his first letter, the apostle John said several tests should be applied:

1 JOHN 2:4–6: *"The man who says, 'I know him,' but does not do what he commands is a liar, and the truth is not in him. But if anyone obeys his word, God's love is truly made complete in him. This is how we know we are in him: Whoever claims to live in him must walk as Jesus did."*

1 JOHN 2:9: *"Anyone who claims to be in the light but hates his brother is still in the darkness."*

1 JOHN 3:6: *"No one who lives in him keeps on sinning. No one who continues to sin has either seen him or known him."*

1 JOHN 3:10: *"This is how we know who the children of God are and who the children of the devil are: Anyone who does not do what is right is not a child of God; nor is anyone who does not love his brother."*

1 JOHN 4:8: *"Whoever does not love does not know God, because God is love."*

1 JOHN 4:15: *"If anyone acknowledges that Jesus is the Son of God, God lives in him and he in God."*

LIFE DOESN'T "JUST HAPPEN"

"We are His workmanship, created in Christ Jesus for good works, which God prepared beforehand so that we would walk in them" (Ephesians 2:10 NASB).

Ever wonder why certain things "just happen" in your life to bless or encourage or guide you, or even give you an opportunity to do something good? It's because

God has planned your days, as the verse above says, so that you have opportunities to do good, help others, and, in a small way, advance God's kingdom on earth!

THE LORD'S PRAYER REVISITED

Have you ever heard little kids recite verses of Scripture and other sayings (like the Pledge of Allegiance)? Over the years, perhaps you've heard some of the hashes kids have made of the Lord's Prayer. Here is a rendition of it using every aberration uttered by kids when reciting it:

"Our Father, who does art in New Haven, Harold (or Halloween) be thy name. Thy king should come, thy will is dumb, or earth as it is in Kevin. Give us this day some dirty bread. And forgive us our bets, as we forgive our bettors. And lead us not into Penn Station, but deliver us from weevils. For thine is the kingdom, the powwow, and the gory forever. Hey-Men!"

We hope you didn't mess it up that badly in your youth, but if you want to see the prayer you most likely heard originally, read Matthew 6:9–13 in the King James Version of the Bible.

A REAL WISE GUY

Considered one of the great kings of the east, Solomon was David's second son by Bathsheba (her first son died by decree of God because of his parents' sin of adultery and murder). He began tremendous building campaigns and built a palace and

Solomon's Temple, one of the seven wonders of the ancient world. When Solomon first became king, God came to him in a dream and offered him a gift: he could have anything he requested—riches, power, whatever. He chose wisdom, and God, because of this excellent choice, gave him riches *and* power. He was known far and wide for his unmatched wisdom.

An example of that wisdom occurred in 1 Kings 3:16–28. Two prostitutes had children, and one of the women accidentally rolled over during the night and suffocated her son. Since her friend was asleep, she switched babies. In the morning, the second woman realized a switch had been made and protested. They were brought before Solomon to solve the dispute. He heard their case, then ordered that the remaining child be cut in half with a sword, so that each woman could have a half. The true mother cried out at that point, saying she'd rather let the thief keep the boy than kill him. The errant prostitute didn't care, though, and said, "He shall be neither mine nor yours; divide him" (v. 26 NASB). It was through this "trick of logic" that the real mother was revealed, and thus Solomon gave her the boy.

The B-I-B-L-E

The word *Bible* comes from the Greek word *biblia*, for "book." The collection of "books" that we know as the Old Testament and the New Testament was called "the Book" in Greek. This happened because people noted it as the first widely published book in human history. More handwritten copies of it became available in the first century and following than any other book.

MEMORIZE, MEMORIZE, MEMORIZE

Memorizing Scripture is a tremendous discipline. If you memorize 1 new verse a week, you will have 52 memorized in a year, 520 in ten years. Imagine what God can do in your life with 520 verses inscribed on your heart! Here are a few to get you started (or perhaps refresh your memory):

PHILIPPIANS 4:13: *"I can do everything through him who gives me strength."*

PSALM 118:1: *"Give thanks to the Lord, for he is good; his love endures forever."*

LAMENTATIONS 3:25: *"The Lord is good to those whose hope is in him, to the one who seeks him."*

THREE IN ONE

Though we call Jesus the "second member of the Trinity" or the Godhead—which consists of the Father, Son, and Holy Spirit—you never find the word *Trinity* in the Bible. Several passages, though, speak specifically of the idea of a Trinity.

The only Old Testament passage where the Bible lists all three members of the Trinity in one concise statement is Isaiah 48:16: "Come near me and listen to this: 'From the first announcement I have not spoken in secret; at the time it happens, I am there.' And now the Sovereign LORD has sent me, with his Spirit." The Trinity is found in the three titles in the verse: "Sovereign LORD," God the Father; "me," Jesus the Son, who is speaking; and "his Spirit," the Holy Spirit.

Several New Testament passages also list the same three persons in one entity:

MATTHEW 3:16–17: *"As soon as Jesus was baptized, he went up out of the water. At that moment heaven was opened, and he saw the Spirit of God descending like a dove and lighting on him. And a voice from heaven said, 'This is my Son, whom I love; with him I am well pleased.'"*

MATTHEW 28:19: *"Go and make disciples of all nations, baptizing them in the name of the Father and of the Son and of the Holy Spirit."*

ROMANS 8:9: *"You, however, are controlled not by the sinful nature but by the Spirit, if the Spirit of God lives in you. And if anyone does not have the Spirit of Christ, he does not belong to Christ."*

1 CORINTHIANS 12:3–6: *"I tell you that no one who is speaking by the Spirit of God says, 'Jesus be cursed,' and no one can say, 'Jesus is Lord,' except by the Holy Spirit.*

There are different kinds of gifts, but the same Spirit. There are different kinds of service, but the same Lord. There are different kinds of working, but the same God works all of them in all men."

2 CORINTHIANS 13:14: *"May the grace of the Lord Jesus Christ, and the love of God, and the fellowship of the Holy Spirit be with you all."*

EPHESIANS 4:4–6: *"There is one body and one Spirit—just as you were called to one hope when you were called—one Lord, one faith, one baptism; one God and Father of all, who is over all and through all and in all."*

1 PETER 1:1–2: *"Peter, an apostle of Jesus Christ.*

To God's elect, strangers in the world, scattered throughout Pontus, Galatia, Cappadocia, Asia and Bithynia, who have been chosen according to the foreknowledge of God the Father, through the sanctifying work of the Spirit, for obedience to Jesus Christ and sprinkling by his blood:

Grace and peace be yours in abundance."

JUDE 20–21: *"Dear friends, build yourselves up in your most holy faith and pray in the Holy Spirit. Keep yourselves in God's love as you wait for the mercy of our Lord Jesus Christ to bring you to eternal life."*

All these passages contain oblique references to the Father, Son, and Spirit as equal in power, authority, and divinity. So it is from these and many others that theologians have come to define the Father, Jesus, and the Spirit as equally divine. This is how we get the teaching of the Trinity.

How is it possible for God to be three persons but not three Gods? Theologians say that God exists as three persons, all distinct and equal, entirely individual and real. However, they all come from the same "essence"—God, which is the name we give to the divinity. Thus, while God exists as these three persons, he is still one God in essence, not three gods, as some accuse Christians of believing.

Ministers have illustrated the idea in various ways. For instance, water can exist as ice, as a liquid, or as a gas (water vapor or steam). These are all water, but it exists in three forms.

Or take an egg. It has a shell, the clear part or albumin, and the yolk. Thus, while the egg is one basic thing, it has three parts.

Others compare the Trinity to human marriage. Here we have two persons who unite and in some sense form a third "persona" between them—"us together."

Nonetheless, each of these illustrations leaves out various aspects of the Trinity. Ultimately, the doctrine of the Trinity is what is known as a true antinomy, the theological idea in which several contradictory elements come together into one unified truth. In the end, nothing in nature or human experience perfectly exemplifies the Trinity, which is as it should be, since God is ultimately far greater and more mysterious than mere human understanding could pin down.

I DIDN'T SAY IT; GOD DID

"We also constantly thank God that when you received the word of God which you heard from us, you accepted it not as the word of men, but for what it really is, the word of God, which also performs its work in you who believe" (1 Thessalonians 2:13 NASB).

The Bible is not the "word of men," as some say, but the "word of God."

If that is so, how should you treat it?

HOW GOD GOT HIS THOUGHTS TO THE WRITERS OF THE BIBLE (1)

Many people wonder how we got the Bible. Some imagine it happened a lot like playing the old game of "telephone." Remember that one? People arranged themselves in a line, the first one whispered a message to the second one, and the second one to the third one, and so on, whisper-whisper, to the end of the line. Then everyone had a good laugh at what the last person thought the first person's message was. Maybe it started out, "Every good boy does fine." But the last gal thought it was, "Evvie's grubby boy loves twine."

What began fairly simply has ended up pretty garbled.

"And that's how we got the Bible," say some. People passed down the stories, added to, subtracted from, babbled, switched, multiplied, and messed them up until someone finally wrote them down and they became part of the "lore" of history. Thus, Moses didn't really part the Red Sea. What actually happened was much simpler. A slave named Moe talked some fellow Jewish slaves into trying to escape the Egyptians, he led them down to the sea, dove in, and ripped across in just a few seconds. Everyone thought it was a miracle. They all jumped in, swam across, and escaped from the evil Egyptians. Later that year, they entered the Olympic relays in Athens and blew everyone away!

Not a bad story, wouldn't you say? Certainly not something as farfetched as God splitting the sea wide open and marching three million Israelites across on dry ground. So you can guess what happened. Around the campfire, in the homestead, at the Sheep Lodge, the descendants of Moe told the story telephone-game fashion, and it began to evolve. One person thought it would be good to give Moe a more respectable name like Moses. Another decided to add the idea that it wasn't just a few slaves but the whole nation of Israel that escaped. A third slipped in the element of the Red Sea. And then someone came up with the idea of God parting it like a comb dividing a beehive hairdo! Presto, we ended up with the story of Moses and Israel's escape from Egypt.

Well, it might happen that way in a parlor game. But that's not how we got the Bible. God—almighty, wise, gracious, and perfectly able to keep track of the facts—wasn't about to let his ideas be changed, added to, jazzed up, or dumbed down by people sitting around campfires and supper tables.

(The next installment of this article is found on page 35.)

SURPRISING SYMBOLS

In the Old Testament, God often used symbols and images to teach us about his real nature; since he is an invisible Spirit, the Hebrews had little idea what he was like. These eight significant symbols used in the Bible help us understand who God is and what he is like.

1. God is the Rock (Deuteronomy 32:4).

2. God is my Shield (Psalm 18:2).

3. God is my Stronghold (Psalm 18:2).

4. God is my Deliverer (Psalm 18:2).

5. God is a Shepherd (Psalm 23:1).

6. God is a Refuge and Strength (Psalm 46:1).

7. God is a Strong Tower (Psalm 61:3).

8. God is like a lion (Isaiah 38:13).

These images speak of protection, safety, security. Above all, God wanted the Hebrews, who were nothing more than nomads in a dangerous world, to feel safe and secure in his hands.

COOL HAND LUKE

Sir William Ramsay, British scholar and archaeologist, had this to say about Luke and his writings: "Luke is a historian of the first rank; not merely are his statements of fact trustworthy . . . this author should be placed along with the very greatest of historians," and "Luke's history is unsurpassed in respect of its trustworthiness."[1]

Here are a few examples of what convinced Sir Ramsey:

- Luke 2:2 cites Quirinius, the supposed governor at the time of the census ordered by Augustus Caesar. Quirinius was known from the Roman records as governor from A.D. 6 to A.D. 9, well after the birth of Christ. We also know from the writings of Hebrew historian Josephus that a census taken in A.D. 6 caused an uprising by the Jews. Since nothing more was known about Quirinius as a governor of Syria, the critics said once again that the Bible was wrong.

  However, a stone fragment found at Tivoli near Rome in 1764 offers an interesting archaeological sidelight on this situation. The inscription on the stone honors a man who was governor of Syria and Phoenicia two times under Augustus, though this official isn't named. Nonetheless, the list of accomplishments inscribed on the stone indicates this person could not have been anyone but Quirinius. He was military governor there while another man named Varus was civil governor.

  This find also corresponds to other records found in Egypt that indicate an earlier census under Augustus occurred in 8 B.C. Since it would normally have taken two to four years for such a process to be carried out, this timing falls completely within the time of Luke's writing.

- The critics said that Luke's statement in Acts 14:1–6 that the cities of Lystra and Derbe were in Lycaonia, and that Iconium was not, was false.

Because of an incorrect statement from Cicero, they believed Iconium was in Lycaonia. However, in 1910 Sir William Ramsay unearthed a monument claiming that Iconium was a Phrygian city, as Luke had said.

- In Acts 19:23–29, Luke wrote of a riot in Ephesus that constituted a "civic assembly" or "ecclesia" in a theater. Critics said no theater could accommodate that many people. Excavations in Ephesus revealed an inscription that mentioned certain silver statues of Artemis (or Diana, the Ephesians' primary goddess). These statues were placed in the theater when a full crowd was gathered (an "ecclesia"). When fully excavated, it was found that this theater could hold more than twenty-three thousand people.

- In Acts 21:28, Luke cites another riot in Jerusalem that broke out because Paul had taken a Gentile into the temple. Critics said that could not have occurred, as there was no law about such things. However, several inscriptions have been found regarding the temple, one of which reads, "No foreigner may enter within the barrier which surrounds the temple and enclosure. Anyone who is caught doing so will be personally responsible for his ensuing death."

- Acts 28:7 refers to Publius, the leader in Malta, who had the title "first man of the island." Critics said such a title was ridiculous. Archaeologists have found inscriptions from Malta, however, that do give him the title of "first man."

- Last, in Acts 17:6, Luke referred to the civil authorities of Thessalonica as "politarchs." Once again, because the classical Greek literature made no such reference, critics assumed Luke was wrong. However, scientists have found some nineteen inscriptions with that very title. In fact, five of the inscriptions specifically refer to Thessalonica itself. One incredible find was of a Roman arch in Thessalonica on which six politarchs are mentioned by name.

THE FACE BEHIND THE VEIL

The "Veil of Veronica" was discovered in Rome in about the twelfth century. It quickly became identified with St. Veronica. The legend surrounding it went like this: As Jesus carried the cross to Golgotha, the hill where he would be crucified, a woman in the crowd named Veronica stepped out onto the Via Dolorosa ("The Way of Sorrows," which is the road Jesus walked along to the hill). She offered him her kerchief so he could wipe the sweat from his forehead. He stopped and took it, then pressed it to his face. He returned the kerchief to her. Later, as Veronica studied the cloth, she saw that Jesus's face had become imprinted upon it.

People added to the legend over the years suggesting that Veronica was the same woman Jesus had healed of a twelve-year-long bleeding problem (see Matthew 9:20–22). Others said she was the wife of Zacchaeus, the height-challenged tax-gatherer who climbed a tree to see Jesus pass by (see Luke 19:1–10). Jesus stopped by the tree and told Zack to come down. Later, he dined at the tax collector's home.

Papal bulls or decrees were issued in 1143 that determined that the bit of cloth be known as the "true image of the Lord," otherwise known as the "Veil of Veronica" because of its association with the legendary St. Veronica.

In time, nearly every church in Europe displayed a reproduction of the veil, though today you cannot find it publicly exposed but must view it through a golden plate, like an icon.

Strangely enough, the face on the veil compares closely to the outline of the image on the Shroud of Turin. Some scholars today believe the veil may have been copied from the shroud. The eyes on it are closed, the chin and outline are long and narrow, and no ears show at the sides. The beard divides into three pieces (although on the shroud there are only two). The scars from Jesus's scourging and crucifixion are quite obvious on both the shroud and the veil. Today, the veil resides in Rome.

Some followers believe this story is true, while others says it's a fake. It appears this is either a fantastic miracle or a rather amazing fabrication by some forger who used secret methods to create the image. It's up to you what to believe.

A HEART ON FIRE

Marguerite Marie Alacoque (1647–90) experienced a vision in which she saw the heart of Jesus aflame with love for humanity. From that, she believed God led her to establish the "Holy Hour" of communion every Friday in the church. She also established the Feast of the Sacred Heart on the Friday following the feast of Corpus Christi (the "body of Christ").

BIBLE PROPHECY ON DISPLAY

Ezekiel prophesied against the island nation of Tyre because of its persecution of Israel in 724 B.C. He said the city would end up as nothing but bare rock where fishermen would spread their nets. This had a couple of fulfillments—the first when Nebuchadnezzar conquered Israel in 586 B.C. and besieged the land-based city from 585 B.C. to 573 B.C. At that time, the people escaped to the island, which ultimately repulsed the attack. Later, in 332 B.C., Alexander the Great destroyed the island city by using the rocks and stones from the earlier destruction on the land to build a causeway to the island. From that, he utterly destroyed Tyre. Today it is a bare rock where local fishermen lay out their nets to dry in the sun, precisely as the prophecy says (see Ezekiel 26:4–5).

BOOKS OF THE OLD TESTAMENT

There are thirty-nine books, which are divided into five sections.

LAW OF MOSES (ALSO, THE TORAH, OR PENTATEUCH)

Genesis

Exodus

Leviticus

Numbers

Deuteronomy

HISTORICAL BOOKS

>Joshua

>Judges

>Ruth

>1 and 2 Samuel

>1 and 2 Kings

>1 and 2 Chronicles

>Ezra

>Nehemiah

>Esther

BOOKS OF POETRY

>Job

>Psalms

>Proverbs

>Ecclesiastes

>Song of Songs

MAJOR PROPHETS ("MAJOR" IN TERMS OF LONGER BOOKS)

>Isaiah

Jeremiah

Lamentations (also written by Jeremiah)

Ezekiel

Daniel

Hosea

MINOR PROPHETS ("MINOR" IN THE SENSE OF SHORTER BOOKS)

Joel

Amos

Obadiah

Jonah

Micah

Nahum

Habakkuk

Zephaniah

Haggai

Zechariah

Malachi

BAD GUYS OF THE BIBLE

Who were some of the worst characters in the Old Testament?

Here are the top sixteen in order of appearance:

1. Cain murdered his brother Abel (Genesis 4:1–15).

2. Lamech vowed to be avenged on anyone seventyfold after committing several murders himself (Genesis 4:24).

3. Pharaoh, king of Egypt, refused to let the enslaved Israelite nation go until his land was devastated by God's miracles (Exodus 5–12).

4. The ten spies wilted before the "giants" in the land of Canaan and led Israel into forty years of wandering (Numbers 13–14).

5. Achan who took items under God's ban illicitly and paid for it with his life and the lives of his relatives (Joshua 7:16–26).

6. King Saul was deposed as king of Israel for his many crimes against God (1 Samuel 9–31).

7. Goliath and his brothers opposed Israel (1 Samuel 17:23–51).

8. King David committed adultery and then murder despite a deep belief and faith in God (2 Samuel 11–12).

9. Amnon, a son of King David, raped his sister, Tamar, then hated her after the rape (2 Samuel 13).

10. Absalom, another son of King David, murdered his brother, rebelled against his father, and tried to take over Israel (2 Samuel 13:23–39).

11. King Solomon, despite being the wisest, richest, and most God-blessed man in history, became an idolator in his last days (1 Kings 10–11).

12. King Ahab was an idolatrous, murderous king of Israel (1 Kings 16:29–22:40).

13. Jonah, a racist prophet, didn't want to see the enemies of Israel converted and given eternal life because of his hatred for them (book of Jonah).

14. King Manasseh was a genocidal, maniacal king of Judah (2 Kings 21:1–18).

15. All of the kings of Israel "did evil in the sight of the Lord" (see 1 and 2 Kings, 1 and 2 Chronicles for a full history).

16. Many of the kings of Judah also "did evil in the sight of the Lord" (see 1 and 2 Kings, 1 and 2 Chronicles for a full history).

"REEDING" AND WRITING THE BIBLE

Many scholars believe that Moses (1520–1400 B.C.) wrote the first five books of the Old Testament, called the Law or Torah. Torah means "law" in Hebrew. These are also called the Pentateuch, which translates to "five books" from Greek.

Most likely Moses wrote on papyrus, a kind of paper fashioned from papyrus stalks. Papyrus is a reed that grows in marshy and boggy areas, on the banks of rivers, and in delta waters. Papyrus makers cut the stalks and lined them up lengthwise to make the front side of a page. Next they did the same with other stalks, lining them up perpendicular to the first group. They pressed and glued the stalks together to fashion the front and back of a whole page. These pages were rather rough, brittle, and would rot in a matter of years. This was why many people chose to write on clay tablets made of wet clay and pressed with a stylus to create various letters before the clay dried. However, more writing could be placed on a piece of papyrus, and thus it was preferred for space and cost reasons. Egyptians invented this kind of paper in about 2000 B.C.

The pages could be lined up and made into a scroll. Scribes and others did this by gluing together flat leaves of papyrus, which were about a square foot in size, and then rolling them into a long coil. A complete book like Genesis would have been fifty or sixty feet long if the scroll was unwound on the ground.

Moses had plenty of time to do this during the forty years that he led Israel in the wilderness. We might picture him sitting in his tent, using a reed he had sharpened and dipped into ink that was made by crushing charcoal and mixing it with water. He may have employed some crude alphabet from that period, perhaps letters from the Akkadian, Ugaritic, or Sinaitic writings. It's possible some precursor of the Hebrew alphabet existed at the time, with its twenty-two letters shaped like small pictures. Archaeologists have shown that such writing was employed at the time of the Mesopotamians from 3000 B.C. So common was writing in Egypt during Moses's life that even women's toilet articles had inscriptions on them. These have been dug up in various places, including the pyramids. Other writings have been found in the Egyptian turquoise mines at Serabit-el Khadim. There, Semitic miners recorded their work and kept notations of building projects on the walls.

Archaeologists have confirmed that the Old Testament relates names, places, peoples, and times with tremendous accuracy. Today, even though we do not have the original documents—they have long perished—we have copies that were passed along through the ages by people who not only committed themselves to precise transcription, but who also believed these documents were from God and should be treated with reverence and the highest respect.

THE FIRST PRINTED BIBLE

The first Bible put together through the use of movable type was printed by Johannes Gutenberg in 1455 in Mainz, Germany. It was written in Latin.

Gutenberg arranged this Bible in three volumes. Many pages were lavishly illustrated with designs and pictures. Today, no one knows how many copies Gutenberg printed. At the time, chapter and verse divisions were unknown. He printed on vellum, a very expensive kind of "paper" from that time. Few people could afford such Bibles but church leaders, kings, governors, and the like. Often, political leaders commissioned printers to produce these fine manuscripts for the nobility.

Today, about forty copies of Gutenberg's series exist, on display in the Library of Congress in Washington, DC, and the British Library in London, England.

EARLY TRANSLATIONS

Scholars today have determined that the whole Bible was written by A.D. 100, the last book, Revelation, being the last one actually written. No other books have been added to this "canon"—the list of books considered the true and only books inspired by God.

Many translations have followed. One of the first, Jerome's Vulgate, a Latin translation from the Hebrew Old Testament and the Greek New Testament, was completed in 405. This became the standard Bible for hundreds of years thereafter as the capital city of the church became located in Rome, where only Latin was spoken. A scholar, Jerome translated directly from the Hebrew and Greek while living in a cave in Bethlehem next to the Grotto of the Nativity, which at the time many believed was the birthplace of Jesus.

Over the centuries, many other translations have been done in more than eighteen hundred languages of the world.

ORIGINAL ENGLISH TRANSLATIONS

Many different English versions of the Bible came into existence during the Middle Ages leading into the Reformation. John Wycliffe, an Englishman, created the first English version. The New Testament appeared in 1380 and the Old Testament two years later. Several scholars helped Wycliffe. His translation was based on the Latin Vulgate versions, not the original languages of Hebrew, Aramaic, and Greek. All the copies were written by hand and thus were extremely expensive and rare. Today about 170 exist in many different museums and libraries.

Other versions in English followed, most notably that of William Tyndale. Born in 1494, from his earliest years he yearned to create a translation of the New Testament that would reach the common people of England. For that purpose he worked and translated, but the church at that time fought against him, believing only priests and churchmen should read the Bible. He was persecuted and finally left England, seeking to find printers in European countries who would put his Bible into print. A printer in Worms, Germany, brought out the first English translation of the whole New Testament in 1525. The printer completed three thousand copies. Quickly, these were smuggled back into England. So successful, accurate, and readable was this version that 90 percent of the King James Version of the Bible employs his precise wording.

Unfortunately, King Henry VIII broke with the Roman Catholic Church in 1534, causing the rise of the Anglican church. Already on the run, Tyndale remained in Antwerp, Germany, in hiding. An English Roman Catholic betrayed him in 1536. He was captured, then tried and condemned to death as a heretic in Germany. He was executed by strangulation and his body was burned at the stake.

Immediately, his translations were banned and burned throughout England. However, his work awakened the king to the need for an English version of the Bible for the common people.

Following Tyndale, other English versions were created: Miles Coverdale's in 1535, Thomas Matthews's in 1537, and the "Great Bible" in 1539, called "Great" because of its large size and lavish illustrations. The Geneva Bible was finished in 1557 and was the first one to incorporate chapters and verses.

The Catholic Church next decided to create its own version to rival the many Protestant translations. This led to the printing of the Rheims-Douai version, completed in 1610. Unfortunately, the translators used the Latin Vulgate, not the original languages, and this version was much inferior as a result.

WE HAVE THE POWER

God has not only created us in his image, but he has also given us a similar power to create. Through that power, the arts, sciences, and all other forms of human work and creation have resulted. While we cannot actually create out of nothing—"ex nihilo"—like God, making physical living things like animals, plants, or other things, we can use the objects of God's creation—paint, rock, music, and so on—to fashion our own objets d'art.

TWENTY GREAT QUESTIONS

Difficult questions aren't unique to contemporary society. Check out these sticky wickets—and their answers—faced by people in the Old Testament.

1. How did the world come to be? (Genesis 1)

2. How did humankind come to be? (Genesis 2)

3. How did evil come into the world? (Genesis 3)

4. When did the first murder occur? (Genesis 4)

5. What happens when people are left entirely to themselves without a sense or concern for God? (Genesis 6–9 [the Great Flood] and Judges)

6. How did the languages of the world come to be? (the story of the Tower of Babel in Genesis 11)

7. Why does God let us go through suffering at the hands of our fellow man? (the story of Joseph in Genesis 37–50)

8. How can we live successfully? (Exodus 20 [the Ten Commandments] and Proverbs)

9. What is God like? (Exodus 32–34)

10. How are we to deal with times when we seek God's blessing and it never seems to come? (the story of Hannah in 1 Samuel 1–2)

11. Why do good people suffer tremendous wrong? (the story of Job)

12. Why does God make us wait? (Psalm 27)

13. Why do unbelievers get rich and prosper? (Psalm 73)

14. How does God want a woman to live? (Proverbs 31)

15. Is there any real meaning in this life? (Ecclesiastes)

16. How does God want a man to live? (Ecclesiastes 7–12)

17. How does God want a husband to treat his wife romantically? (Song of Songs)

18. How does God feel about people who reject him? (Hosea)

19. Does God care about the heathen? (Jonah)

20. Why doesn't God do anything about evil in the world? (Habakkuk)

HOW GOD GOT HIS THOUGHTS TO THE WRITERS OF THE BIBLE (2)

In our first installment, we looked at one process many believe was used to give us the Bible. We compared it to the modern "telephone game."

Other people believe we received the Bible through certain members of the tribe memorizing the whole history of the people and reciting it on appropriate occasions and holidays. Kind of a "tribe scribe" deal with one smart fellow passing on the history to his disciple, generation to generation, until one of them learned to write and put pen to papyrus and wrote it all down.

Remember that scene from the famous book *Roots*, where Alex Haley visited an African tribe he believed was descended from his ancestor Kunta Kinte? Haley listened to the tribe "historian" recite the story of his people. The story began at the very beginning because that was how the historian had memorized it, and he had no way of starting in the middle or zipping to the right part like a DVD player. So the people sat for hours as he recited it. Haley almost fell asleep several times, but then came that serendipitous moment when he heard the man say the name Kunta Kinte. The historian related how white people from a ship captured Kunta along with others and then disappeared forever.

Haley's heart pounded as he realized this was the tiny piece of heart-stopping information he needed to prove where his family came from.

So is that the way the Bible was passed on before it was written down? A special historian with a great memory bank kept it in his head, passed it on to apprentices, and then when writing was invented, someone finally wrote it all down on bricks, clay tablets, or whatever they happened to have available at the time?

Memorization is good, a powerful medium, but human memory is faulty at best. If God had had to rely on human memory, his plan to get his Word into our hands surely would have failed. How many times have you memorized something—a telephone number, a joke, a bit of gossip—only to find important details elude you at the punch line? People tend to "remember" differently than what really happened, and the desire to embellish is terrific, to say nothing of the possibility of major mistakes.

(See the third installment in this continuing article on page 53.)

TWISTED SCRIPTURE

Leaders in Christian Bible memory and training programs for kids in churches have heard some strange quotations of Scripture from their students. Here are some samples:

MATTHEW 5:5: *Blessed are weak, for they shall inhabit the earth . . .*

MATTHEW 16:24: *If anyone wants to follow Jesus, he must destroy himself and get up on the cross . . .*

MATTHEW 18:11: *For the Son of Man has come to reek and to rave at those who are lost . . .*

MATTHEW 18:20: *For wherever two or three are gathered in Jesus's name, someone spills his milk . . .*

MATTHEW 19:24: *It is easier for a rich man to go through the eye of a needle, than for a camel to get into the kingdom of God . . .*

LUKE 4:4: *It is written, Man shall not live to be dead alone, but on every bird that comes out of the mouth of God . . .*

LUKE 10:27: *You shall love your labor as yourself . . .*

JOHN 3:16: *For God so loved the world he gave his only forgotten Son . . .*

1 CORINTHIANS 15:4: *And that Jesus was buried and he's a rose again . . .*

JAMES 2:10: *For whoever shall keep the whole Law and gets stumbled in one point . . .*

JAMES 5:16: *Confess your sins to one another so that you may be beat up . . .*

REVELATION 2:4: *I have this against you, that you have left your first glove . . .*

YOU HAVE IT ALL!

Thank God for all the elements of yourself that are a reflection of his image:

Looks—you're beautiful, unique, special.

Intellect—with it you can learn and understand virtually anything.

Abilities—they win you respect and give you something to achieve.

Emotions—they make living worthwhile.

Will—gives you power to freely choose to do right your whole life.

Five senses—with them you experience God's world.

Spirit—it's the part of you that "sees" and "feels" God.

Power to do good—it gives the same kind of satisfaction and joy that God feels when he works in the world.

KING JAMES'S GREATEST ACHIEVEMENT

In 1607, King James I of England, successor to Queen Elizabeth I, ordered biblical scholars to create a new English translation of the Bible. He didn't like any of the translations available at the time (such as the Geneva Bible) and thought this might be a way to leave a legacy to his kingdom. As a result, he gathered forty-seven of the best Greek and Hebrew scholars in England to produce it. These men were divided into six teams, three for the Old Testament, two for the New Testament, and one for the Apocrypha. This group finished the King James Version (KJV) in just two years and nine months. It was printed in 1611.

It became a sensation, partly because of its beautiful and poetic English but also because of its accuracy. It remains even today the quintessential Bible for the English-speaking world, despite the fact that other versions have attempted to supplant it. Its one flaw may be that it is based on the "Textus Receptus" (TR)—the "received version"—which was considered the authentic Greek Bible, copied from the original documents. Many scholars today dispute that the TR should be employed as the best version of the Greek New Testament, mainly because a number of earlier texts have been discovered that in some places disagree with the TR. The dispute rages today in many schools and seminaries, some believing the KJV is "God's version" and others claiming newer translations based on the "Critical Text," the text put together by various scholars from the many earlier documents we now have at our disposal, are better.

THE ROYAL FAMILIES

Who were the kings of Israel and Judah?

UNITED KINGDOM	
SAUL	1 Samuel 9–10
DAVID	1 Samuel 16–31; 2 Samuel 1–24
SOLOMON	1 Kings 1–11

DIVIDED KINGDOM—ISRAEL

JEROBOAM	1 Kings 11:26–14:20	led rebellion against Rehoboam in south
NADAB	1 Kings 15:25–28	son of Jeroboam
BAASHA	1 Kings 15:27–16:7	killed Nadab
ELAH	1 Kings 16:6–14	son of Baasha
ZIMRI	1 Kings 16:9–20	killed Elah, who was drunk
OMRI	1 Kings 16:15–28	built Samaria, the capital
AHAB	1 Kings 16:28–22:40	son of Omri, killed in battle
AHAZIAH	1 Kings 22:40–2 Kings 1:18	oldest son of Ahab
JEHORAM	1 Kings 3:1–9:25	youngest son of Ahab
JEHU	2 Kings 9:1–10:36	ended line of Ahab
JEHOAHAZ	2 Kings 13:1–9	Jehu's son; army wiped out by Syrians
JEHOASH	2 Kings 13:10–14:16	Jehoahaz's son; defeated Judah in war
JEROBOAM II	2 Kings 14:23–29	Jehoahaz's son; Jonah worked during his reign
ZECHARIAH	2 Kings 14:19–15:12	Jeroboam's son; killed by Shallum
SHALLUM	2 Kings 15:10–15	reigned one month; killed by Menahem
MENAHEM	2 Kings 15:14–22	extremely brutal king
PEKAHIAH	2 Kings 15:22–26	Menahem's son; killed by Pekah
PEKAH	2 Kings 15:27–31	killed by Hoshea
HOSHEA	2 Kings 15:30–17:16	dethroned and imprisoned by Assyrians

DIVIDED KINGDOM—JUDAH

REHOBOAM	1 Kings 11:43—12:24	son of Solomon; started civil war with north by stupidity
ABIJAH	1 Kings 14:31—15:8	Rehoboam's son; defeated Jeroboam
ASA	1 Kings 15:8–14	Abijam's son; first godly king for Judah
JEHOSHAPHAT	1 Kings 22:41–50	Asa's son; godly king; allied with Ahab
JEHORAM	2 Kings 8:16–24	Jehoshaphat's son; married to Athaliah, daughter of Ahab and Jezebel
AHAZIAH	2 Kings 8:24–9:29	Jehoram's son; killed by Jehu
ATHALIAH (QUEEN)	2 Kings 11:1–20	took over after death of Ahaziah; killed all royalty except one
JOASH	2 Kings 11:1–12:21	son of Ahaziah; hidden from Athaliah
AMAZIAH	2 Kings 14:1–20	son of Joash; killed in conspiracy
UZZIAH	2 Kings 15:1–7	son of Amaziah; struck with leprosy
JOTHAM	2 Kings 15:32–38	son of Uzziah; built temple's gate
AHAZ	2 Kings 16:1–20	son of Jotham; sacrificed son to pagan god
HEZEKIAH	2 Kings 18–20	son of Ahaz; reformer
MANASSEH	2 Kings 21:1–18	son of Hezekiah; Judah's worst king
AMON	2 Kings 21:19–26	son of Manasseh; killed by servants
JOSIAH	2 Kings 22:1–23:30	son of Amon; reformer
JEHOAHAZ	2 Kings 23:31–33	son of Josiah; deposed by Egypt and taken there
JEHOIAKIM	2 Kings 23:34–24:5	Josiah's son; burned Jeremiah's scroll; enslaved by Babylonians
JEHOIACHIN	2 Kings 24:6–16	Jehoiakim's son; carried to Babylon
ZEDEKIAH	2 Kings 24:17–25:30	uncle of Jehoiachin; blinded and taken into exile[2]

THE MUSLIM NEXT DOOR

"Help, my new next-door neighbor is a Muslim!"

Statisticians report that somewhere between two and five million Muslims live in the United States today. These people are not all of Arab descent; many are African Americans and others who have become Muslims as adults.

However, more and more Arab-descended Muslims are entering the United States, and their populations in the Middle East grow continually. Muslims practice the religion of Islam, which is now the world's second largest religion after Christianity, with more than a billion followers worldwide.

What does the Bible say to those of us who find our new neighbors are Muslims? Are we to fear them? Ostracize them? Welcome them?

Since Islam did not exist until more than five hundred years after the last books of the New Testament were written, the Bible says nothing specifically about this religion. However, the Bible says much about the stranger, foreigner, and person visiting us from other countries and creeds.

For instance, God commanded his people, the Jews, to appreciate and even love aliens.

Deuteronomy 10:18–19, states, "He defends the cause of the fatherless and the widow, and loves the alien, giving him food and clothing. And you are to love those who are aliens, for you yourselves were aliens in Egypt."

In Psalm 146:9 we learn that God "watches over the alien and sustains the fatherless and the widow, but he frustrates the ways of the wicked."

God wanted Israel to welcome aliens because the Israelites experienced such welcome when they first lived in Egypt during the time of Jacob and Joseph (see Genesis 46 and following).

When outsiders disputed legally over some issue with an Israelite, Moses ordered the judge to be fair: "I charged your judges at that time: Hear the disputes between your brothers and judge fairly, whether the case is between brother Israelites or between one of them and an alien" (Deuteronomy 1:16).

In the New Testament, Jesus also received outsiders regardless of their race or creed. Jesus didn't even require that the person believe in him or become one of his disciples. Jesus conversed with a Syrophoenician woman whose daughter was demon-possessed in Mark 7:25–30:

As soon as she heard about [Jesus], a woman whose little daughter was possessed by an evil spirit came and fell at his feet. The woman was a Greek, born in Syrian Phoenicia. She begged Jesus to drive the demon out of her daughter.

"First let the children eat all they want," he told her, "for it is not right to take the children's bread and toss it to their dogs."

"Yes, Lord," she replied, "but even the dogs under the table eat the children's crumbs."

Then he told her, "For such a reply, you may go; the demon has left your daughter." She went home and found her child lying on the bed, and the demon gone.

Jesus also made a hated Samaritan the hero of his well-known parable of the good Samaritan. The Samaritans originally were Jews conquered by the Assyrians in 722 B.C. These Jews intermarried with their captors and became Samaritans. Pure Jews from the south considered them half-breeds. A Pharisee or highly religious Jew in Jesus's time would travel extra miles to go around rather than the shorter way—through—Samaria, the home of these tainted half-Gentile, half-Jewish people. The Jews hated the Samaritans and considered them enemies.

The parable, found in Luke 10:25–37, was Jesus's ultimate answer to this prejudice: "Love your neighbor as yourself." When asked, "Who is my neighbor?" Jesus told the story of the kind Samaritan who alone helped a beaten Jew, while other Jewish leaders purposely avoided him.

"Who is my neighbor?" we ask Jesus. He replies, "Anyone and everyone. Love them all."

Bible believers must love Muslims, treat them justly, and deal with them fairly in all situations. Why not regard that local Muslim family as folks who need a welcome and the kind of love you can give? Take them over a cake or pie. Let them know you care. Ninety-nine percent of Muslims are people who care about their faith and who want to do good. Just because a few "bad apples" live in our world does not mean we should reject or be suspicious of all of them.

CREATION CONTROVERSY

The evolution/creation controversy continues to rage, but look at these remarkable similarities in the following comparison:

DAY	CREATION	EVOLUTION
DAY 1	"Let there be light"	beginning: Big Bang
DAY 2	Earth and heavens	billions of years ago: first matter
DAY 3	vegetation	millions of years ago: one-celled organisms, vegetation
DAY 4	sun, moon, and stars	various distant stars still forming
DAY 5	fish and birds	millions of years ago: fish, reptiles
DAY 6	mammals, animals	6 million years and less: mammals and land animalsl
DAY 6	humankind	1 million years and less: humankind

Even if you don't accept the theory of evolution, which many Christian theologians, scientists, and leaders don't, this template shows astonishing agreement, especially if you recognize God's "days" don't necessarily refer to twenty-four-hour days, and day four above proposes a problem we still haven't solved. However, when you consider the Bible's explanation and the era in which it was offered—prescience—it makes far more sense than most other creation scenarios.

SLEEPLESS IN THE MONASTERY

The Acoemetae ("sleepless ones") were a monastic order who lived during the fifth century. The monks were divided into choirs and practiced round-the-clock singing without intermission year-round.

MIRACLE EAR

When Peter lopped off a slave's ear, Jesus picked it up and healed it on the spot. This is what happened:

As the soldiers, led by the enemies of Jesus, arrived in the Garden of Gethsemane to take him prisoner, a disciple saw what could happen, and he cried, "Lord, should we strike with our swords?"

Jesus didn't answer in time, and he struck the servant of the high priest, whacking off the servant's right ear. Jesus immediately shouted, "No more of this!" And he touched the man's ear and healed him (Luke 22:49–51).

From other passages, we know Peter swung the sword that cut off the ear, and the name of the injured servant was Malchus (see John 18:10).

GOD TOLD ME TO TELL YOU . . .

Following is a list of the writing prophets of the Bible along with when they ministered and what they did. As you can see, the prophets' messages don't appear chronologically in our Bibles.

1. Obadiah (850–840 B.C.) prophesied against Edom, Israel's enemy.

2. Joel (835–796 B.C.) prophesied to Judah.

3. Jonah (784–774 B.C.) preached in Nineveh of impending disaster and led the city into the greatest revival in biblical history.

4. Amos (763–755 B.C.) warned of injustice and evildoing in Israel.

5. Hosea (755–710 B.C) worked in Israel, the northern kingdom, before they were conquered in 722 B.C. by Sennacherib.

6. Isaiah (739–680 B.C.) prophesied and ministered to the people of Judah.

7. Micah (735–710 B.C.) spoke to Judah of their sin.

8. Nahum (650–630 B.C.) prophesied against Nineveh of their evildoing.

9. Zephaniah (635–625 B.C.) encouraged Judah just before their exile to Babylon.

10. Jeremiah (627–570 B.C.) worked with the king and people of Judah, preparing them for their exile to Babylon in 586 B.C.

11. Habakkuk (620–605 B.C.) questioned God about his justice in light of Judah's sins and learned how God would deal with the evildoers.

12. Daniel (605–536 B.C.) ministered to the exiles in Babylon.

13. Ezekiel (593–570 B.C.) worked with the exiles in Babylon.

14. Zechariah (520–470 B.C.) encouraged Judah after their exile and return to Israel.

15. Haggai (520–505 B.C.) reminded Judah of their need to rebuild the temple after their return from Babylon.

16. Malachi (437–417 B.C.) preached against wrongs in the new nation long after their return from Babylon.

BOOKS OF THE NEW TESTAMENT

The New Testament comprises twenty-seven books and writings by the disciples ("learners") and apostles ("sent ones") of Jesus Christ. These books are accepted by the Christian church worldwide as the final word of God to the world before Jesus comes back again to begin his eternal kingdom. It is New in contrast to the Old, and it is a Testament in that it represents God's final covenant or agreement with humankind. It is considered the unique, eternal, and supernatural revelation of God through his Spirit to all who will come near and listen. In it are four divisions:

GOSPELS ("GOOD NEWS")

>Matthew

>Mark

>Luke

>John

HISTORY

>Acts

EPISTLES

>Romans

>1 and 2 Corinthians

>Galatians

Ephesians

Philippians

Colossians

1 and 2 Thessalonians

1 and 2 Timothy

Titus

Philemon

Hebrews

James

1 and 2 Peter

1, 2, and 3 John

Jude

PROPHECY

Revelation

LONG LIVE THE QUEEN

The book of Esther tells her story.

About 473 B.C., Xerxes (called Ahasuerus in the King James Version) threw a great banquet for his nobles. They all got so drunk that the king called on his queen,

Vashti, to show her great beauty off before them. It may be that he wanted her to undress, although that is not clear. She refused, and immediately Xerxes was advised to depose her.

To find a new queen, a contest followed. One of the Jews of the realm, Mordecai, decided to get his beautiful cousin Esther into it. She ultimately won and became the new queen. What follows in the book is a kind of providential chess match between Satan and God as Satan tries to engineer the destruction of the Jews in Babylon through the prime minister, Haman. One day, while being honored by the king, Haman rode down the street. All bowed to him except Mordecai the Jew. Haman soon found out who Mordecai was and of his race. As a result, not knowing that Esther was Jewish because she had hidden it from all involved, Haman, in a deep rage, went to the king and talked him into decreeing a certain day when all non-Jewish people could murder the Jews and take their possessions. Mordecai soon found out about this plot and warned Esther, telling her to talk to the king about this dastardly scheme.

At first Esther balked, but Mordecai showed her that she may have risen to the queenship because of this very problem, because it would be through her that the nefarious plot was stopped. Esther called on her people to fast and pray. After several days, she decided to walk into the throne room of the king—risking her life, because no one was allowed to come in unsolicited—and ask him to come to a banquet in his honor.

The time came, and Esther stepped before the king, not knowing what he would do. This was especially risky for her because she, though queen, hadn't seen the king for nearly a month and thought she might have gone out of favor. This would be the perfect opportunity for him to get rid of her if that was what he desired.

Nonetheless, the king admitted her and agreed to come to her banquet—along with Haman—where she would reveal her true request. At the banquet, Esther was about to reveal her heritage and concern about the new law, but something in her heart (providence) stopped her. Instead, she asked the king to come to a second banquet with Haman again, where she would tell him her request. At the same time Haman built a glorious gallows on his property that he intended to hang Mordecai on.

That night the king couldn't sleep and asked that the records of his kingdom be read to him, presumably to help with his insomnia. While listening, he learned of how Mordecai had found out about a plot to assassinate the king and warned the leaders of it. The plot was foiled, and Mordecai forgotten until that night. The king asked what honor had been bestowed on Mordecai and found out that nothing had been done. He decided to use the first person who came into the court that morning to honor Mordecai.

The first man in was Haman, and he was sent to honor Mordecai in a way most embarrassing, with him leading the horse through the city and yelling for all to honor the man on it. When Haman went home, he was told things had gone against him and he'd better watch out.

He went to Esther's banquet with the king, and there Esther revealed the plot against the Jews. The king made a new decree, allowing the Jews to fight back against anyone who followed the old law. Haman was hanged on the gallows he built for Mordecai. And Mordecai became "second to the king" in the land.

The story of Esther is one of God's providential work to rescue his people from the claws of the enemy, ultimately Satan. All through the book, various "coincidences" occur that lead to a good outcome for God's people. Without once mentioning the name of God, the book shows how God works behind the scenes in our lives to stop the machinations of our enemies and to promote us in the world and bring good into our lives.

WHAT YOU NEED IS WHAT YOU'VE GOT!

"Grace and peace be multiplied to you in the knowledge of God and of Jesus our Lord; seeing that his divine power has granted to us everything pertaining to life and godliness" (2 Peter 1:2–3 NASB).

Note the remarkable truth of this verse: God's power has given us "everything" we need for "life and godliness." In effect, Peter is saying nothing that happens to us in life is beyond God's power in us. Do you believe that?

JUST FOR PUN

1. Where was tennis played in the Bible? "Joseph served in Pharaoh's court."

2. Is there baseball in the Bible? Yes, for "in the big inning, God . . ."

3. What kind of car did Adam and Eve have? "God drove them out of the Garden of Eden in a Fury."

4. What kind of car did the disciples ride in? "The disciples were together in one Accord."

5. Who was the smallest person in the Bible? "Bildad the Shu-hite."

6. Who was even smaller than Bildad? "The wicked flea."

7. Who was the greatest comedian in the Bible? Samson—he brought down the house.

8. What did Adam tell the kids was the reason he had to leave the Garden of Eden? "Because your mother ate us out of house and home."

9. Who had no parents in the Bible? Joshua, the son of Nun.

10. Why couldn't the family play cards on the Ark? Because Noah was always standing on the deck.

And one for the show:

11. Who makes the coffee in the morning according to the Bible? "He-brews."

HOW GOD GOT HIS THOUGHTS TO THE WRITERS OF THE BIBLE (3)

In the first two installments of this continuing article, you remember we talked about the process of how the writers of the Bible received God's word. The "telephone game" method was debunked, and then the Haley's *Roots* idea was shown to be false. Here's another more recent idea.

In the late 1800s, scholars offered a theory called the "Documentary Hypothesis." Julius Wellhausen, a German scholar, proposed this idea about how the first five books of the Bible (known as the Law of Moses) came to be. Wellhausen posited that Moses couldn't have written these books alone, or even in his time. Writing didn't even exist. The Hebrews possessed no workable alphabet. The stories picture traditions that couldn't have existed in those times. And some of the tales, they suggested, smacked of a half-crazed jester simply trying to please the king with exaggerated stories of the king's ancestors simply to ward off the axe. (Wellhausen wasn't exactly a "fundamentalist"!) Thus, he proposed that a person called a "redactor" (one who "wrote it down" or an editor) collected various and sundry "writings, musings and thoughts" from several story and idea lines in Jewish history. He lived around 800 B.C., and he was a committed Jew, a good writer, and a man with an imagination.

This person, after gathering the documents together, thought, "Why don't I just weave this into one big book?" He began "redacting" all the data and soon arrived at the five books of the Bible that until then most people believed had been written by one person, Moses. This redactor selected his material from four basic story lines he'd discovered in his collection. These were later labeled J-E-D-P for short. These story lines included:

- stories involving a God named Jehovah, otherwise known as J

- stories by a God named Elohim, who was E

- laws and rules on the basis of a Deuteronomist or collector of the Law, known as D

- rituals and rites involving Priestly codes and rules about Hebrew religion—P

The "Documentary Hypothesis" theorized that through these four lines, J-E-D-P, the redactor invented the first five books of the Bible—Genesis, Exodus, Leviticus, Numbers, and Deuteronomy. This redactor possessed such wisdom and craft that sometimes he combined material from all four lines into one story or even one verse. At other times, he just used a story from one line (like the creation in Genesis 1) and then followed it up with another story from another line (the "other creation" in Genesis 2). Followers of Wellhausen even produced books in four colors highlighting the four woven pieces so that as you read, you could see which pieces were pulled from where.

This hypothesis appealed to so many scholars and leaders in the late nineteenth century that many Christians bought into it. Even today, it is taught in major seminaries, despite the fact that archaeological discoveries from the twentieth century have discredited the premises on which the hypothesis was built, as well as the whole idea of a redactor and four different documents. Archaeologists have since discovered that writing existed all the way back to the Sumerians and other cultures—over a millennium before Moses! The Jews created a Semitic alphabet long before Moses was ever born! Many of the "weird" stories and traditions (like Sarah giving Abraham her handmaiden, Hagar, to "raise up a son") have been confirmed from other local cultures existing in Abraham's and Moses' day. And just because a story seems miraculous or supernatural doesn't mean it couldn't have happened! Today, it is inconceivable that Moses, educated in all the lore and history of the Egyptians, would not have been able to read and write. And there is no basis on which to say he made the whole thing up. Egyptian history confirms many of the stories we find in these books.

(See the next installment of this article on page 71.)

ME, MYSELF, AND I

The Bible says nothing directly about cloning. Such technology did not exist in biblical times. Even today, there's much question as to whether cloning is possible. So far efforts have proved less that satisfactory.

So what does the Bible say indirectly about cloning?

We know that God fashions us with his own hands in the womb. He personally sculpts our bodies and souls. Psalm 139:13–16 tells us,

For you created my inmost being;
*   you knit me together in my mother's womb.*
I praise you because I am fearfully and wonderfully made;
*   your works are wonderful,*
*   I know that full well.*

My frame was not hidden from you
  when I was made in the secret place.
When I was woven together in the depths of the earth,
  your eyes saw my unformed body.
All the days ordained for me
  were written in your book
    before one of them came to be.

These verses indicate that God personally designs us to the point of laying out our lives in some ultimate plan. Would not cloning, where an original cell from the host is placed in a woman's womb, receive the same treatment from God? Wouldn't God fashion that person as if it were just a twin or duplicate, which we know is possible now? If so, then wouldn't a clone be a true human, with all the rights and privileges of a free being?

In a passage in the New Testament, we find another thought: "Do you not know that your body is a temple of the Holy Spirit, who is in you, whom you have received from God? You are not your own; you were bought at a price. Therefore honor God with your body" (1 Corinthians 6:19–20).

Wouldn't a clone be capable of housing the Spirit of God like any other person? Then how is a clone different from anyone else, except that it did not come from a fertilized egg by the usual means?

Of course, with so little to go on, it's impossible to say just what God might tell us concerning cloning. But it appears from the passages cited that grave problems could result: people born without souls, possibly; rich people using clones for body parts so they can live longer; building up a population of warriors by cloning great fighters, and so on. The idea of cloning people in order to get organs for replacement is sheer cannibalism at its worst and unjust at best. For if a clone is a real human being, no matter how his birth came about, he should be given all the normal rights and privileges of humanity, not turned into a flesh mill.

THE TEN AMENDMENTS

Answers from seventh graders on questions about Moses and the Ten Commandments:

"Moses led the Hebrews to the Red Sea, where they made unleavened bread, which is bread without any ingredients. The Egyptians were all drowned in the dessert. Afterward, Moses went up on Mount Cyanide to get the ten amendments."

"The first commandment was when Eve told Adam to eat the apple. The fifth commandment is to humor thy father and mother. The seventh commandment is thou shalt not admit adultery."

JESUS SAID HE WAS . . . WHAT?

Jesus referred to himself ten times in the New Testament as "I am . . ." something. Here is a list of what those statements were, and their meanings.

1. Jesus told the woman at the well point-blank that he was the Messiah. She tried at first to dismiss him by saying that when the Messiah came, he would

explain everything to the people. In response, Jesus told her, "I who speak to you am he." He revealed his divinity and purpose—and that he was the Messiah (John 4:26).

2. Jesus called himself the "bread of life." The staple of life in Jesus's time was bread. When he said he was the Bread of Life, he used the symbol to show he is the most basic thing every person needs to live. Jesus is the sustainer of life itself (John 6:35).

3. Jesus revealed to his listeners that he is the "light of the world." Jesus made this statement after saving the woman caught in adultery from being stoned. In a world shrouded in darkness, Jesus came to light the path, to show the way. As the Light of the World, he is the one who guides individuals to heaven (John 8:12).

4. Risking everything with his critics, Jesus used the great Old Testament words that God gave Moses as his name: "I am," saying that before Abraham existed, "I am!" The Hebrew word, "Yahweh," means "I am who I am," or the "self-existing one," the one who needs nothing to sustain himself but is eternal, all-powerful, and all-knowing. When Jesus said this to the Jews, they understood he was claiming equality with God (John 8:58).

5. When Jesus wanted to make plain how a person could enter the kingdom of heaven, he said he was the "door." You enter a room through a doorway.

Similarly, you enter the kingdom of God through another kind of door, a person—Jesus. Here, he clearly showed that if anyone wanted to enter heaven, the kingdom of God, he could only come through belief in Jesus himself (John 10:7 NASB).

6. To those who understood sheepherding very well, Jesus used the image, saying he was the "good shepherd." The picture of the shepherd guarding, feeding, guiding, and protecting his sheep is found throughout Scripture, but this was the first time Jesus identified himself as a shepherd. Through this statement he inspired trust in his listeners. They could feel they were safe if they gave their lives to him (John 10:11).

7. A group had spent days mourning Lazarus's death, but Jesus showed he was "the resurrection and the life." He said this to Lazarus's sister Martha who had gone to Jesus and told him if only he'd been there, her brother would have lived. Jesus spoke these great words in response. He confirmed that he had the power to raise the dead, no matter how long he had been in the grave. Seconds later, he actually did raise Lazarus from the dead (John 11:25).

8. When Thomas wanted to know how to follow Jesus into heaven, Jesus told him he is "the way and the truth and the life." Jesus spoke these words at the Last Supper. The disciples feared losing him and wanted to go wherever

he was going. He told them to have faith, for he was the way (the path there), the truth (the one they could trust absolutely), and the life (the source of eternal life) (John 14:6).

9. A vine carries water and nutrients from the ground to the grapes growing on it. The vine provides all that is needed. Without it, the grapes couldn't exist. Jesus illustrated that his disciples, like grapes, had to depend on the vine for all their nourishment, telling them he himself was the "vine." They couldn't do anything without his help and support (John 15:5).

10. In his final words to John in the book of Revelation, Jesus used the Greek alphabet to show he is eternal, the one who begins (alpha is the first letter) and who also ends everything (omega is the last letter). Jesus encompasses all time and space, and there is nowhere that he isn't. He is the "Alpha and Omega," master of the beginning, the end, and all in between (Revelation 22:13).

Jesus used these ten statements to help his disciples understand his role in their lives, his identity as the Messiah, and his power to sustain them throughout life. The disciples saw that Jesus was the true Source of all they needed. Depending on him became the essence of what it meant that he was their shepherd, the vine, the resurrection and the life, and so on.

WHY BOTHER?

Why did God create the universe if he knew what the invasion of evil would do to it? The Bible reveals he continued in his plan despite the risks for several reasons:

1. He wanted to include us in the joyous adventure of life (Jeremiah 31:3).

2. Through the intrusion of evil, he would teach each of us many great truths about himself and ourselves (1 Corinthians 13:9–12).

3. He wanted to show and teach the angels of his glorious person and power (Ephesians 3:10).

4. He knew he would ultimately redeem it—at the cost of the death of his Son—and make it possible for it to become utterly glorious (Hebrews 9:23–28).

5. As Creator, he must create or deny a basic capacity he has (Revelation 4:11).

And that's only the beginning.

WHY WAIT?

Throughout human history, singles have been suckered into giving up their virginity for fine-sounding words that usually turned out to be hollow lies. Many young people have awakened to this truth and have chosen to wait for the right person, the person they marry, rather than give the precious gift of their virginity to the first guy or girl who says, "I love you."

The Bible calls us to purity—in our relationships, in our sexual habits, in the very words we express with our tongues. Solomon warned in the book of Proverbs about the "adulteress," the woman who tempts a young man into having illicit sex (see Proverbs 5). He says later of adultery, "A man who commits adultery lacks judgment; whoever does so destroys himself" (Proverbs 6:32). The seventh commandment, "You shall not commit adultery" (Exodus 20:14) warns against the practice of any kind of sexual immorality, not just extramarital relationships.

In the New Testament, we find a strong word in Hebrews 13:4: "Marriage should be honored by all, and the marriage bed kept pure, for God will judge the adulterer and all the sexually immoral."

Abstinence, though, goes even further. For the young woman or man contemplating marriage, it offers the opportunity to give your partner the pure gift of yourself, untouched by any other person. That's a high calling in our world of free love and sex. It means you offer your body and soul to another for the first time on your wedding night.

For those who choose this path, God says he applauds and honors them. Their lives will be blessed.

What about the person who cannot seem to control his or her sexual desire? The Bible's answer to that is marriage. Paul advised both men and women, "To the unmarried and the widows I say: It is good for them to stay unmarried, as I am. But if they cannot control themselves, they should marry, for it is better to marry than to burn with passion" (1 Corinthians 7:8–9).

The Bible never condones sexual promiscuity or any sexual relations outside of marriage. Abstinence keeps single people from contracting STDs, from hurting themselves emotionally, and from becoming entangled in abusive relationships. Many young people today speak happily of the power of abstinence in their lives and how abstinence truly does offer a great reward in God's eyes. You discover you are pleasing God as well as preserving for your future mate a precious gift.

Choosing abstinence is a logical and wise path to take. While our sexual desires remain strong, taking that route, no matter how difficult, is always the self-honoring and God-honoring choice.

TOP TEN BAD GIRLS OF THE OLD TESTAMENT

In order of the seriousness of the sins they committed:

1. Jezebel, queen to King Ahab of Israel, was an idolater whose wicked schemes led her husband into gross sin (1 Kings 16:29–21:25).

2. Athaliah, a murderous queen, almost killed off the line of the Messiah through King Solomon (2 Kings 11), but one heir was saved by the high priest and became king after her death.

3. Delilah seduced Samson and led him into ruin (Judges 16).

4. Gomer was the prostitute prodigal wife of Hosea, about whom he wrote a love story portraying God's love for idolatrous Hebrews (Hosea 1–3).

5. Tamar seduced her father-in-law, Judah, by pretending to be a temple prostitute (Genesis 38). She became pregnant and bore twins, Perez and Zerah. Perez is in the genealogy of Jesus.

6. Eve, the first woman, led her husband, Adam, into sin by eating of the "forbidden fruit." However, she was merely deceived; her husband rebelled against God knowingly (Genesis 3).

7. Rahab, a prostitute, lived in Jericho at the time it was destroyed (Joshua 2) but became a woman of faith and is mentioned as a member of the line of Christ (Matthew 1:5).

8. Miriam, sister of Moses, rebelled against his leadership and was punished by God with leprosy, which was later healed at Moses's request (Numbers 12).

9. Michal mocked her husband, King David, when he celebrated at the bringing of the ark of the covenant into Jerusalem (2 Samuel 6:16–23) and was left childless of David as a punishment.

10. Penninah, second and less-loved wife of Elkanah, mocked and treated the first wife, Hannah, with contempt because of Hannah's barrenness. She made Hannah's life miserable (1 Samuel 1).

WHERE IT ALL BEGAN

Remarkably, scientists believe the "cradle of civilization" began in exactly the area of the earth described in Genesis 2:10–14. While other cultures have spun stories that center creation in their time and place, the Bible once again takes a view that agrees with all we have discovered today about history.

JESUS HAD A LOT TO SAY ABOUT . . .

Jesus is the most quoted individual in history, yet *Bartlett's Familiar Quotations* doesn't even list him. The following are some of his best-known quotes (besides those already listed under Wit and Wisdom of Jesus):

On being salt in the world: "You are the salt of the earth. But if the salt loses its saltiness, how can it be made salty again? It is no longer good for anything, except to be thrown out and trampled by men" (MATTHEW 5:13).

On being insulted: "Do not resist an evil person. If someone strikes you on the right cheek, turn to him the other also" (MATTHEW 5:39).

On trying to serve God and money: "No one can serve two masters. Either he will hate the one and love the other, or he will be devoted to the one and despise the other. You cannot serve both God and Money" (MATTHEW 6:24).

On seeking wealth and riches: "Seek first his kingdom and his righteousness, and all these things will be given to you as well" (MATTHEW 6:33).

On worry: "Do not worry about tomorrow, for tomorrow will worry about itself. Each day has enough trouble of its own" (MATTHEW 6:34).

On his mission: "It is not the healthy who need a doctor, but the sick" (MATTHEW 9:12).

On evangelism: "I am sending you out like sheep among wolves. Therefore be as shrewd as snakes and as innocent as doves" (MATTHEW 10:16).

On discipleship: "Come, follow me, and I will make you fishers of men" (MARK 1:17).

On his purpose: "The Son of Man came to seek and to save what was lost" (LUKE 19:10).

On taxes: "Give to Caesar what is Caesar's, and to God what is God's" (LUKE 20:25).

On God's love: "God so loved the world that he gave his one and only Son, that whoever believes in him shall not perish but have eternal life" (JOHN 3:16).

On worship: "God is spirit, and his worshipers must worship in spirit and in truth" (JOHN 4:24).

On his coming back: "Do not let your hearts be troubled. Trust in God; trust also in me. In my Father's house are many rooms; if it were not so, I would have told you. I am going there to prepare a place for you" (JOHN 14:1–2).

On peace: "Peace I leave with you; my peace I give you. I do not give to you as the world gives. Do not let your hearts be troubled and do not be afraid" (JOHN 14:27).

On God's Word: "Sanctify them by the truth; your word is truth" (JOHN 17:17).

A FIRST-CENTURY POLITICAL RADICAL

Simon the Zealot was one of Jesus's disciples. He was a Zealot, meaning "person of great zeal" or "political passion." The Zealots were a Jewish political party who fought against Rome in A.D. 6 with a leader known as Judas the Galilean (see Acts 5:37). They opposed paying taxes to Caesar because they considered it treason against God. After their defeat in A.D. 6 the group survived for another sixty years but was never able to muster a strong opposition again.

Simon joined Jesus's just-forming group of disciples, perhaps because he believed Jesus would bring in the revolution his friends so longed for. Or maybe for other reasons. What we do know is that Jesus convinced him that God can change the world, not through killing, but through love and goodness in the people who will follow him. No one knows anything more about this man; however, his commitment to Christ was unquestioned. That became the real revolution for Simon (see Luke 6:15; Acts 1:13).

THE LAST WORDS OF JESUS ON THE CROSS

In order, these are the seven last statements Jesus spoke from the cross:

To the Roman soldiers and the crowd gathered to watch him die: "Father, forgive them, for they do not know what they are doing" (LUKE 23:34).

To the repentant thief crucified on the cross next to him: "Today you will be with me in paradise" (LUKE 23:43).

To his mother, Mary, and his disciple John: "Dear woman, here is your son. . . . Here is your mother" (JOHN 19:26–27).

To God, his Father: "My God, my God, why have you forsaken me?" (MATTHEW 27:46).

To the Roman soldiers: "I am thirsty" (JOHN 19:28).

To the crowd: "It is finished" (*Tetelestai,* the word written across a prisoner's sentence posted to his cell door in Roman prisons when his sentence was concluded) (JOHN 19:30).

To his Father: "Father, into your hands I commit my spirit" (LUKE 23:46).

A LONELY ROAD

The court where Pilate tried Jesus was called the "Gabbatha" (John 19:13), or "Stone Pavement." For many centuries, no proof of its existence surfaced, and critics claimed it was one proof of the New Testament's lack of credibility as authentic history. However, William F. Albright, Johns Hopkins University professor and archaeologist, has proven that this court was in the Tower of Antonia, where the Roman military headquartered in Jerusalem. It had been buried during the rebuilding of Jerusalem in the time of Hadrian but was discovered recently by Albright.[3]

A REFLECTION ON THE POOL

Critics claimed that this site of Jesus's healing of the lame man in John 5 was one more myth from the New Testament. However, excavations near the Church of St. Anne in 1888 unearthed the pool and located it in the northeast quarter of the old city (the area called Bezetha, or New Lawn).

AN ACTUAL OFFICIAL

In Romans 16:23, Paul mentioned a city leader named Erastus. As usual, critics cited this as a misnomer. However, on a limestone slab near a theater in Corinth, archaeologists unearthed part of the pavement with an inscription. It said, "Erastus, in return for the aedileship [a Roman magistrate who had charge of the temple of Ceres, a god], laid the pavement at his own expense." Many scholars believe this was the same person written up by Paul, although no one can be absolutely sure.

COINING A PHRASE

Excavations over the years have found several different kinds of coinage that existed in Jesus's time and are mentioned in the New Testament.

1. The tribute coin, cited in Matthew 22:17–21 and several other passages, called in Greek the *denarius*, was the same kind that Jesus asked to be held up when the Pharisees and Herodians challenged him about paying taxes. A small silver coin, Caesar's image was stamped on the face. It was worth about one day's wages for a common laborer.

2. The "thirty silver coins" paid to Judas Iscariot to betray Jesus (Matthew 26:14–15) was probably the same as thirty shekels. A shekel weighed two-fifths of an ounce. It became a silver coin of about the same weight.

3. The widow's "very small copper coins" ("mite" in the King James Version) from Mark 12:41–44 used a Greek term, *lepta*, for "copper coins" and the Roman term *quadrans* for "penny." It was the smallest copper coin valued today at only a "fraction of a penny" as the New International Version cites it.

HOW GOD GOT HIS THOUGHTS TO THE WRITERS OF THE BIBLE (4)

If we didn't get the Bible by means of a "telephone game" methodology, Alex Haley's *Roots* idea, or Wellhausen's "Documentary Hypothesis," then how did we get it?

If you're like me, you probably believe the Bible is God's Word, the message from God to humankind that contains truth from beginning to end. Thus, the stories and history contained in it can't be garbled versions of the originals or anything close to legends, myths, or the product of the mind of a supposed redactor. If the Bible is made up or messed up or even mixed up, we're all in big trouble.

Just a casual reading of the Bible shows that it's good writing and solid storytelling that relates one basic tale from beginning to end: how God created the world, how it became corrupt and evil, how he fixed the invasion of evil, how he finally sent his Son who solved the basic problem of human sin and judgment, and how in the end evil will be vanquished and confined to a pit from which it can never escape. If you want to put it all in one simple sentence, the Bible is about the redemption of humankind from the power of sin and evil.

The Bible, if you study it closely, veers very few times from that story. Study the sacred texts of other religions and you often find a strange mishmash of philosophy and rules, rules, rules, many of which have no seeming theme or meaning. But amazingly enough, though the Bible features more than forty writers who wrote during a fifteen-hundred-year period, it still possesses astonishing internal agreement, sports few major problems and contradictions, and keeps driving the same point home: believe in God, and he will help you straighten out your life, experience salvation, and inherit eternal life.

How could a huge book like this keep so closely to that theme? Few preachers can stick with one idea in a twenty-minute sermon! How could all those preachers in the Bible make sense for thousands of pages?

It's also astonishing that where the Bible touches on subjects like science, archaeology, medicine, and so on, it consistently sticks to what we know is true about our world today. Other than in the creation story (which we looked at earlier), amazingly few statements in the Bible contradict what we know today about the world and the universe.

Take something like the idea that the world is flat. If the Bible said such a thing, we'd be quite right in throwing it away. But it never does, even in the oldest passages, where people like Moses and Samuel could not possibly have known the nature of our world and the universe as we know them today. Instead, the Bible says rather plainly these things about us and our planet:

- All people are descended from one man and woman (Adam and Eve in Genesis 1 and 2).

- The world began with a Big Bang. God said, "Let there be light!" (Genesis 1:3).

- The idea of a worldwide flood, destroying humankind, is found in most cultures. Anthropologists have discovered that almost all cultures have a flood story in their lore and history (Genesis 6–9).

- Modern languages are derived from a single original tongue (Tower of Babel episode, Genesis 11).

- The earth is hung on blank space. "He spreads out the northern skies over empty space; he suspends the earth over nothing" (Job 26:7).

- The earth is round, even spherical. "He sits enthroned above the circle of the earth, and its people are like grasshoppers" (Isaiah 40:22).

- The stars are without number and far away. "I will make the descendants of David my servant and the Levites who minister before me as countless as the stars of the sky and as measureless as the sand on the seashore" (Jeremiah 33:22). And, "Is not God in the heights of heaven? And see how lofty are the highest stars!" (Job 22:12).

Amazingly enough, even Genesis 1:1–31, the story of the creation, follows the basic outline that evolutionists propose brought humankind into being. To be sure, there are vast differences, but when you compare that to what other ideas have been proposed in human history, it's uncanny how the Bible and modern knowledge agree.

You would think if the Bible contained just the writing of humans with great imaginations, all kinds of weird notions about the world and the universe would have found place in it. But instead, the Bible cites these facts in a time when scientific knowledge was minimal. How did the writers know these things? Why didn't they tell us crazy ideas like the world is flat or if you travel far enough by sea you will fall off the earth—as many people believed in ancient times?

Why doesn't the Bible posit comical medical practices like, "To cure the chicken pox, kill a chicken, whirl it over your head three times, shout John 3:16, and then have the person with the chicken pox take the chicken to bed for three nights straight (without cooking it and eating it)"?

Because of one very simple truth: it's all from one mind, the mind of God, who knows everything, everywhere and everyhow. The Bible is not just another human book, and humans didn't write their own opinions or ideas or made-up beliefs in it. Rather, they received the truth from God. How? By a process we call revelation.

(Read about revelation in the next installment on page 102.)

KEEPING SECRETS

"The secret things belong to the LORD our God, but the things revealed belong to us and to our children forever, that we may follow all the words of this law" (Deuteronomy 29:29).

As this verse indicates, the Bible wasn't written to satisfy our curiosity, but to change our lives. Certain secrets belong only to God. The rest is for us—to enjoy, to love, to build our lives on.

If you want to read more about the details of the "doctrine of revelation and inspiration," try these books:

- *Knowing Scripture* by R.C. Sproul

- *Foundations of Christian Faith* by James Montgomery Boice

- *1001 Bible Questions Answered* by William L. Pettingill

- *30 Days to Understanding the Bible* by Max Anders

SIGNS OF THE (END) TIMES

In Matthew 24 Jesus gave his disciples some signs that he said would precede his second coming:

1. People coming in the name of Christ, claiming to be Christ: "For many will come in my name, claiming, 'I am the Christ,' and will deceive many" (v. 5).

2. Numerous wars and rumors of wars: "You will hear of wars and rumors of wars, but see to it that you are not alarmed. Such things must happen, but the end is still to come. Nation will rise against nation, and kingdom against kingdom" (vv. 6–7).

3. Famines and earthquakes: "There will be famines and earthquakes in various places. All these are the beginning of birth pains" (vv. 7–8).

4. Persecution of Christians: "You will be handed over to be persecuted and put to death, and you will be hated by all nations because of me" (v. 9).

5. Apostasy, or the turning away of many from the true faith: "At that time many will turn away from the faith and will betray and hate each other" (v. 10).

6. False prophets: "And many false prophets will appear and deceive many people" (v. 11).

7. Lack of love between people: "Because of the increase of wickedness, the love of most will grow cold" (v. 12).

8. The message of Christ preached in all the world: "This gospel of the kingdom will be preached in the whole world as a testimony to all nations, and then the end will come" (v. 14).

9. The Antichrist declaring himself to be God incarnate: "When you see standing in the holy place 'the abomination that causes desolation,' spoken of through the prophet Daniel—let the reader understand" (v. 15).

10. A time of great distress: "Then there will be great distress, unequalled from the beginning of the world until now—and never to be equaled again. If those days had not been cut short, no one would survive, but for the sake of the elect those days will be shortened" (vv. 21–22).

This is a complete list of the things Jesus said would happen before He returned to earth as King and Victor.

SINCERELY, JESUS

This letter was supposedly written by Jesus from heaven. According to the legend, it was found eighteen miles from Iconium, a city of Asia Minor, fifty-three years after Jesus's crucifixion. The legend also says it was originally found under a large stone at the foot of the cross and taken from there to its resting place near Iconium. Engraved on the stone were the words "Blessed are they that shall turn me over." The letter itself read, "The Commandments of Jesus Christ. Signed by the Angel Gabriel, seventy-four years after our Savior's birth." Here are some excerpts from the letter:

Whoever worketh on the Sabbath shall be accursed. I command you to go to church and keep the Lord's Day holy, without any manner of work. . . . I advise you to fast five days in the year, beginning with Good Friday and continuing the four Fridays following. . . . You shall diligently and peaceably labour in your respective callings wherein it has pleased God to call you. . . . He that hath given to the poor shall not be unprofited. . . . He that hath a copy of the letter, written with my own hand and spoke with my own mouth, and keepeth it without publishing it to others, shall not prosper, but he that publisheth it to others shall be blessed of me. . . . Whosoever shall have a copy of this letter and keep it in their house, nothing shall hurt them, and if any woman be in child-birth and put her trust in me, she shall be delivered of her child. You shall hear no more of me but by the Holy Spirit until the Day of Judgment.

This letter, according to history professor Robert Priebsch of London, was written originally in Latin about A.D. 590 in Ebusa, near Spain, on one of the Balearic Islands in the Mediterranean Sea. It was presented to Bishop Vincentius, who passed it on to his people. He immediately sent a copy to Licinianus, bishop of Cathagena, who summarily denounced it as a forgery and fake.

Every now and then it surfaces in some writings, but is immediately denounced by most scholars as a nefarious fraud.

NAKED WORSHIPERS

Adamites lived at various times in history and believed that true worship could only be performed while naked. They were extremely promiscuous as a result and believed that Christ somehow came among them as they worshiped him in the nude.

"MAGIC" BREAD

In the Middle Ages, many weird beliefs arose about the bread used in the Eucharist (or "Lord's Supper"). Some said it possessed magical power, could cure various fevers, make a man sexually potent, and hide criminals from discovery. John Lake (1624–1689), bishop of Chichester, wrote as a result that people often stole the bread from churches. "Witches, sorcerers, charmers, enchanters, dreamers, soothsayers, necromancers, conjurers, cross-diggers, devil-raisers, miracle-doers, dog-leeches and bawds" were primary suspects for the thefts, which they used in their arts and ceremonies.

THE *C* WORD

The word *Christian* is first found in Acts where Luke wrote, "The disciples were called Christians first at Antioch" (Acts 11:26). It was meant as an insult, because it means "Little Christ," like we might say today, "Oh, he's a little Babe Ruth" or "she's a little Madonna" of someone aspiring to be a great personage but failing in the endeavor completely. King Agrippa used the word in Acts 26:28, where the apostle Paul attempted to persuade him to convert to faith in Christ. He said to Paul, "Do you think that in such a short time you can persuade me to be a Christian?" He may have meant it as an insult in the way someone might say, "Do you think I would ever become one of them?"

JESUS IN THE HOUSE

We find thirteen recorded appearances of Jesus to his followers after his resurrection. In their order:

1. To Mary Magdalene—John 20:11–18

2. To the other women—Matthew 28:9–10

3. To the soldiers who saw the stone rolled away (it is not clear what they saw, so this one is speculative)—Matthew 28:11–15

4. To Peter—Luke 24:34; 1 Corinthians 15:5

5. To two disciples traveling to Emmaus—Luke 24:13–32

6. To ten assembled disciples—Luke 24:36–49; John 20:19–25; 1 Corinthians 15:5

7. To the eleven assembled disciples—John 20:26–31; 1 Corinthians 15:5

8. To seven disciples while fishing—John 21:1–25

9. To more than five hundred disciples at one time—1 Corinthians 15:6

10. To the eleven disciples in Galilee—Matthew 28:16–20

11. To James, Jesus's half-brother—1 Corinthians 15:7

12. To the disciples in Jerusalem—Acts 1:3–8

13. To the disciples at his ascension—Luke 24:50–53; Acts 1:9–12

THE YEARS OF THE BIBLE

The Old Testament begins with Creation, when God made the heavens and the earth, the plants and animals, and finally Adam and Eve. The story moves through history to the time of Malachi, the last prophet of Jewish times, who wrote around 450–400 B.C. The Old Testament touches on many different events in history, including the fall of the tower of Babel, the powerful kingdoms of Assyria, Babylon, Greece, and Rome, and several marvelous stories of the lives of saints who did things in the outside world beyond the borders of Israel (Joseph, Ruth, Esther, Job, Daniel).

The ultimate purpose of the Old Testament was to tell Jewish history, its rises, falls, trials, and tribulations. With that in mind, Genesis quickly moves from world history in chapters 1–11 to Jewish history in chapter 12, chronicling the exploits of Abraham and his children. The story follows in Exodus about Moses's leadership and Israel leaving slavery from Egypt and traveling to "the land of milk and honey." We see the rise of the later leaders and judges (in Joshua and Judges) to the beginning of governments run by kings (from King Saul to the last king of Judah, Jehoiakim, before the exile to Babylon in 586 B.C.). After that, we see Jewish history in the books of Ezra, Nehemiah, and Esther.

The Old Testament ends with the prophecy of Malachi, who told the people to await the coming of the Messiah.

The Old Testament doesn't tell a happy story either. It records many of the sins and errors of the first believers, including Noah, who got drunk and lay naked in his tent after the great flood; Abraham, who lied about his wife, Sarah, saying she was his sister; and King David, who committed adultery with Bathsheba and then had her husband murdered. It tells of intrigue, jealousy, anger, lust, and hatred, as well as love, goodness, joy, and peace.

In contrast, the New Testament covers primarily the life of Jesus (in the Gospels) and the early church (Acts). The last book, Revelation, written around A.D. 95, describes a future time of struggle and the eventual second coming of Jesus Christ (although there are many scholars who believe Revelation was fulfilled in A.D. 70, when Jerusalem was destroyed by the Romans).

Like the Old Testament, the New Testament tells how it really was. Thus, we find Peter walking on water with Jesus and then sinking because he lost faith at the last second. In Acts we meet Saul (later known as Paul), who attacked and persecuted the first Christians because he believed they were heretics from the true Jewish faith. We also see him marvelously converted while on the Damascus road. He becomes the greatest missionary in Christian history, traveling all over the Roman Empire and spreading the news about Jesus.

The Bible is a very personal book. It tells it like it is, whether we like it or not!

GONE, GONE, GONE

What does God do with our sins, according to the Old Testament?

1. He separates them from us "as far as the east is from the west" (Psalm 103:12).

2. He cleans up all the stains of sin and makes us white as snow (Isaiah 1:18).

3. He throws them "behind [his] back" (Isaiah 38:17).

4. He "remembers [them] no more" (Jeremiah 31:34).

5. He crushes our sins into the dirt (Micah 7:19).

6. He hurls them into the ocean (Micah 7:19).

Clearly, God meant to convey the fact that a believer receives a forgiveness that is complete and eternal.

HOW GOD WROTE THE BIBLE WITHOUT PEN AND INK

How God gave us the Bible you read today is an amazing adventure. He used the hands, hearts, and minds of prophets, apostles, scribes, translators, and plain folks to write the Bible. It took over a thousand years to write the Old Testament (from about 1400 B.C., beginning with Moses, to about 400 B.C., ending with Malachi). The whole New Testament came together in less than sixty years, from A.D. 40 to about A.D. 100. God used a three-step process to communicate the Bible to humankind: (1) revelation, (2) inspiration, and (3) translation.

1. *Revelation.* For the first step, revelation, God was in direct contact with a prophet, apostle, or leader who recorded God's words. This is different from modern "revelations," which some Christians believe happen today but are not considered as authoritative as the Bible. Most scholars believe the Bible became complete with the last book of the New Testament, Revelation. Revelation is from the word *reveal.* Through it (the process, not the book), God revealed things he wanted known: laws (like the Ten Commandments); prophecies of the future (like in Daniel and the book of Revelation); stories and historical events (like Creation, Adam and Eve, the Tower of Babel), and anything else that a prophet could not learn through study, reading, or other sources.

2. *Inspiration.* When a prophet or apostle received a revelation, he wrote it down in a scroll, on papyrus, or in another format that would preserve it. Inspiration is the process God used to make sure what this person wrote was accurate, and that he didn't embellish or add his own thoughts to it. Inspiration means "God-breathed," for the words themselves were the very breath and voice of God. As a prophet wrote what God revealed, God the Holy Spirit led, guided, and helped him write it with perfect accuracy. Often, the

person not only wrote down what God had revealed directly to him, but also what he learned through research (see Luke 1:1–4) and study. This did not harm the process, though, because God through his Spirit, made sure what the prophet said was accurate, as 2 Timothy 3:16 says: "All scripture is inspired by God and profitable" (NASB). Readers of those first documents could trust them as the very word of God, without error and flawless.

3. *Translation.* The Bible was originally written in Hebrew, Aramaic, and Greek. Most of today's readers don't know those languages and thus could never read the Bible. But God also raised up scholars after the original manuscripts were penned to translate them into modern languages. Jerome, an early scholar who lived from A.D. 345 to 419, translated the Bible from the original languages into Latin. Over the centuries, others have supplied translations, including William Tyndale (Old English) and Martin Luther (German). The standard in English became the King James Version of the Bible, published in 1611, the result of years of research by forty-seven scholars. Today, many other versions are available, including modern paraphrases as well as reader-friendly translations.

LOADING THE OLD TESTAMENT "CANON"

The history of how the thirty-nine books of the Old Testament were collected and recognized as from God himself begins with Moses, who wrote the first five books.

From Moses to the time of Christ, the Jews collected and classified the books. Different rabbis argued about the books over the years, whether they were truly from God. For instance, Esther was disputed because God is never mentioned in the whole book. Some thought Proverbs couldn't be inspired, because of certain contradictions they found in it. Many thought Ecclesiastes shouldn't be included because the author seemed to have no faith until the very last chapter. Many other books existed throughout the years that were simply discarded, though some were collected in the middle section of the Bible, called the Apocrypha.

The books of the Old Testament that we recognize today were never put together in one volume until shortly after the life of Christ. Everything was settled in A.D. 90. At the Jewish Council of Jamnia, all the leading teachers and scholars gathered to determine what the "Testament" or "Covenant" should be. Arguments were heard. At the end, the only books in dispute—Esther, Ecclesiastes, Proverbs, and the Song of Songs—were all summarily declared authoritative and inspired by God.

At that time the whole collection became "canon." This word (pronounced "cannon") could be translated, "measuring rod," and it came to mean the "standard," in the same sense that the length of a foot or a yard is "standardized" by the U.S. government. When scholars talk about the "canon of Scripture," they mean the whole collection of books that conform to certain standards of doctrine, dogma, faith, truth, and integrity.

In the New Testament, we find several references to two basic divisions of the Old

Testament Scriptures recognized in the first century: "Moses" or the Law, and "the Prophets." On one occasion, Jesus spoke of "Moses, the Prophets and the Psalms" (Luke 24:44). We take this to prove that by the time of Jesus, the Hebrews had a definite series of books in mind when they spoke of "Scripture."

The Jews divided the books of the Old Testament three ways: the Law of Moses, the Prophets, and "the writings." These three categories included all thirty-nine books we know today as the Old Testament.

How do we know for sure that the books we have in our Bible are the ones truly given to us by God?

Over the centuries, scholars have devised certain "tests" to determine its authenticity. What are these tests?

First, was the book inspired by the Holy Spirit? That is, did the believing Jews and the early church recognize from the very beginning that these words had the supernatural stamp of God's mind and truth?

Second, was the writer one of the prophets? Do we know anything about the writer's personal history that makes him a person we can trust as a valid prophet of God?

Third, was the book accepted as inspired and authoritative from the time it first appeared and repeatedly throughout history? Did the rabbis and leaders of the church claim the texts as God's word and did they spread the texts abroad, copying and using them in messages, sermons, and books they wrote?

Every book faced these three tests. Throughout history, both the Jewish leaders and the fathers of the Christian church have agreed that these thirty-nine books and only those books are the very word of God. Many other books were discarded along the way because

1. It was obvious the text—because it was full of errors or fantastical, weird, strange, or incomprehensible—could not be from God. Read any of these, such as Belt the Dragon or Ecclesiasticus, books and you will find them very strange indeed, lacking the clarity, vision, and power of the true Word of God.

2. Second, it was clear the book was written well after the time of Christ and thus could not have been written by an apostle.

3. Third, they were rejected by the early church fathers repeatedly and without apology.

What of the Apocrypha? If you have a Catholic Bible of any kind, you will find in the middle between the Old Testament and New Testament a series of books called the Apocrypha, which means, "hidden things" in Greek. The Roman Catholic Church at the Council of Trent in 1545 declared seven of these books as canonical. However, none of the Jewish synagogues or Protestant churches have proclaimed these seven (or another eight, which you will also find in other Bibles) as truly from God. Protestants regard them merely as "human" writings that contain some valuable history (like 1 and 2 Maccabees), but little more.

THEY GOT AWAY WITH MURDER!

A double murder.

A husband kills his wife and then his children.

A gang shoots up a neighborhood and kills an innocent child in the shootout.

What does the Bible offer to the people immediately affected by evil and injustice in our world? It's easy to turn to the trial of O. J. Simpson and other notorious cases and point out that there's no justice in this world. How should we as believers react to this?

The Bible tells us to deal justly with all people (see Romans 13). We are to owe no one anything but love, according to Romans 13:8. God requires all believers to be just in all their dealings. When asked what God most wanted from his people, the prophet Amos said, "Let justice roll on like a river, righteousness like a never-failing stream!" (Amos 5:24). Asked the same question, Micah answered, "He has showed you, O man, what is good. And what does the LORD require of you? To act justly and to love mercy and to walk humbly with your God" (Micah 6:8).

But while justice is an ideal to reach for, the Bible clearly recognizes our world is full of injustice. Human justice is limited. Even the most unprejudiced courts abound with wrong verdicts and sentences. Criminals go free. Sometimes the innocent are wrongly punished. God does not choose to right every wrong and punish every criminal at the time of their crimes. As one person has written, "God does not settle all his accounts on the same day."

What does the Bible say to those who have experienced injustice—a teacher showing partiality, a bully beating up an innocent, a young man getting shot in a drive-by?

For one thing, the Bible validates people's using the law of the land to secure their rights. Paul appealed to Caesar when he was imprisoned unjustly, something any Roman citizen could do. When the leaders of the Jews told the apostles to stop proclaiming the gospel, they said, "Judge for yourselves whether it is right in God's sight to obey you rather than God. For we cannot help speaking about what we have seen and heard" (Acts 4:19–20). Clearly, the Spirit of God, in crafting the Bible, gave us strong guidelines for seeking justice in our world.

But that is not the end of it. We can use the resources of the world all we want, and sometimes we will never get real justice—in the here and now. To such people, the Bible is even more of an assurance. God promises to be with those people and to help them endure in this world. Many examples abound of people whom God greatly blessed but who were also abused by the system. Joseph in Genesis 37–50 remains a prime example, but what about Jesus ending up crucified after a mock trial, or Paul taking the bite of the whip numerous times just because he proclaimed the gospel to Greeks and Romans? The Bible counsels us to be patient, to look to God, and to wait expectantly for his resolutions to such crimes. God repeatedly assures us that at the end of time there will be a great time of judgment (see Revelation 20). Then, God will accomplish complete and perfect justice for everyone who has ever lived. All wrongs will be righted, and all evil properly and righteously punished.

At the final judgment the secrets of all people will be exposed before all creation: "This will take place on the day when God will judge men's secrets through Jesus Christ, as my gospel declares" (Romans 2:16).

Another passage declares that even a person's deepest motives will become evident to everyone at this judgment: "Judge nothing before the appointed time; wait till the Lord comes. He will bring to light what is hidden in darkness and will expose the motives of men's hearts. At that time each will receive his praise from God" (1 Corinthians 4:5).

Still a third passage says God keeps books that record every thought, word, and deed of every individual. All people will answer for each of these on a day in the future, sometimes called the "great white-throne judgment" in Revelation 20:12–13: "I saw the dead, great and small, standing before the throne, and books were opened. Another book was opened, which is the book of life. The dead were judged according to what they had done as recorded in the books. The sea gave up the dead that were in it, and death and Hades gave up the dead that were in them, and each person was judged according to what he had done."

The Bible often reminds us that harsh words, evil motives, and godless deeds will all be exposed at God's final accounting. So, clearly, even though criminals sometimes escape human justice, they will not escape God's. So God is who we are to look to for ultimate justice.

For those who commit evil deeds and think they've gotten away with them simply because they weren't indicted, or who evaded trial through "technicalities," God's word is, "One day you will stand before me, too, and answer for everything."

But to those who deal justly and show love and do good, believing in the Christ of the Bible, God assures us they also will be rewarded for their goodness.

In God's plan, no one gets overlooked. No one is forgotten. No hurt will be left unbandaged. And no evil unpunished.

PREACH IT!

Jesus preached eight lengthy discourses in the Gospels, plus many other extended lessons he gave as teachings.

Sermon on the Mount (Matthew 5–7)

Sending of the apostles (Matthew 10)

Primary parables (Matthew 13)

Instructions on various issues (Matthew 17:24–18:35)

Woes on the Pharisees (Matthew 23)

Olivet Discourse (Matthew 24–25)

Parables of the lost sheep, coin, and son (Luke 15)

Upper-Room Discourse (John 13–17)

NAMES OF GOD

In the Bible, God reveals himself through various names. Each one offers some truth or principle about himself. There are sixteen specific names that God used in the Old Testament.

1. Elohim reflects God's power and might, which shows he can protect us (Genesis 1:1).

2. Jehovah, a word used for Yahweh, speaks of salvation (Genesis 2:4).

3. El-Elyon, "The LORD Most High," demonstrates that he is utterly holy and removed over us in infinite power and perfection (Genesis 14:17–20).

4. El-Roi, "God is strong and sees," proves that he knows our situation in any circumstances and can save us in it (Genesis 16:12).

5. El-Shaddai, "God Almighty," shows that he is the almighty God, all-powerful and able to do anything, even the impossible (Genesis 17:1).

6. Jehovah-Jireh, "The LORD who provides," was coined by Abraham when he went on the mountain to sacrifice his son Isaac. It shows God's power to provide and meet our needs (Genesis 22:13–14).

7. Jehovah-Rapha, "The LORD your healer," signifies his power to heal and help (Exodus 15:26).

8. Jehovah-Nissi, "The LORD our banner," points to the fact that God will lead us out into battle and go ahead of us and behind us (Exodus 17:15).

9. Jehovah-Maccaddeshem, "The LORD your sanctifier," indicates God can transform and consecrate us to his service and worship (Exodus 31:13).

10. Jehovah-Shalom, "The LORD is peace," signifies the fact that God alone can give us peace (Judges 6:24).

11. Jehovah-Rohi, "The LORD my shepherd," speaks of God's leadership and guidance in the paths of life (Psalm 23:1).

12. Jehovah-Sabaoth, "The LORD of hosts" or armies, pictures God's might and power to rescue us from danger and fight on our behalf (Isaiah 6:1–3).

13. El-Olam, "The everlasting God," speaks of the fact that God can never die; he is eternal (Isaiah 40:28–31).

14. Jehovah- Tsidkenu, "The LORD our righteousness," says he is righteous and just on our behalf and to the whole world (Jeremiah 23:6).

15. Jehovah-Shammah, "The LORD who is present," demonstrates that God will be present for us when we need him (Ezekiel 48:35).

16. Adonai means "Lord," representing God's overarching relationship with us (Malachi 1:6).[4]

THAT'S AN ORDER!

How did the Old Testament get into its present arrangement?

Throughout history, scholars have discovered various organizing systems for the thirty-nine books of the Old Testament—chronological, spiritual, or for memorization purposes. Jews generally referred to the divisions as the Law, the Prophets, and the writings. They often grouped certain books together—Jeremiah and Lamentations, Ruth and Judges, and the twelve "minor prophets"—as single books, even though today Christians know them separately. In A.D. 400 the Jewish Talmud first spoke of the books in the order we find them in today's Hebrew Bible.

However, the Christian Bible is markedly different in its order (though not in content). In A.D. 170 a church father named Melito of Sardis went to Israel for the express purpose of authenticating the canon of the Old Testament. He ended up with the thirty-nine books in nearly the same order we have them today in the English Bible. Other church fathers often listed the books in other lineups, but eventually the order we see today became the standard.

Ultimately, when Gutenberg printed the first Latin Bibles in Mainz, Germany, in 1454, the order he used became the pattern for all succeeding Christian Bibles.

DRAWING THE BIBLE

A Sunday school teacher spoke about the birth of Jesus in the manger, and she asked her class of young children to draw pictures of the event. One little boy proudly showed his depiction, and the teacher quickly reeled off the things she recognized: "Why that's the stable, and that's Mary and Joseph, and that's the manger, and those are the shepherds, and here are the kings." But then she found herself looking at a squarish object on legs. Flummoxed, she finally asked, "What is this?"

"Oh, that's their television," the little artist replied.

• • •

In another Sunday school class, the children were asked to draw some of the people from the life and times of Jesus. One child got the disciples right, and Mary and Joseph, and quite a few others. But as the teacher watched him draw, to her surprise the boy depicted a plane with a man in a helmet in the cockpit. "Who's this?" she asked.

"That's Pontius the Pilot," the boy responded.

Still another Sunday school teacher asked her students to draw something from the Bible. All the children set to it, and as the teacher canvassed the room, she stopped in front of a little girl drawing what looked to be the beginning of some handsome, great king. "Who's this?" she asked.

"God," the little girl answered.

Always concerned to teach the truth, the woman said, "No one knows what God looks like."

The girl looked up and smiled. "They will when I get done."

A boy set to drawing a picture of something from the book of Exodus. When he finished, he showed his teacher a recognizable drawing of ten men in army uniforms with modern guns, grenades, and all kinds of fierce weaponry. "Who are these?" asked the teacher, wondering what in the book of Exodus this could refer to.

"The Ten Commandoes," the boy answered.

PLAGUED BY PLAGUES

In the book of Exodus, Moses recorded ten plagues God sent on the nation of Egypt to persuade Pharaoh to let the Israelites go. At first these plagues seem simply to be extraordinary acts and miracles for no reason other than to irritate the Egyptians. However, studied more closely, with a little Egyptian history and religion thrown in, we find that each plague specifically embarrassed one of Egypt's revered idols. God used the plagues not only to show his power and prove his greatness, but he also proved that the Egyptians' gods had no power against him, and thus that he, the God of the Jews, was the one and true God of all.

Here is a list of the miracles and the specific Egyptian gods that were humiliated and shown to be impotent in the process:

MIRACLES	EGYPTIAN GOD
1. Nile turned to blood (7:20)	Hapi, the Nile River god
2. frogs in the land (8:6)	Heqt, frog god
3. gnats (8:17)	Hathor, insect god
4. flies (8:24)	Shu, Isis, fly god
5. diseases on cattle (9:6)	Apis, god of cattle
6. boils (9:10)	Sehkmet, god of health
7. hail (9:23)	Geb, god of sky
8. locusts (10:13)	Serapis, god of the locusts
9. darkness (10:22)	Ra, sun god
10. death of firstborn sons (12:29)	Pharaoh, considered a god himself

PONTIUS PILATE CRASHES

Pilate has been called tactless, hot-tempered, and weak in ruling; to cover his weakness he often resorted to brutal acts. He sent his soldiers to massacre innocent Galileans (see Luke 13:1) and for this reason the Roman government ultimately fired him.

When Jesus stood before Pilate, Pilate tried to get Jesus off the charges and sent home. His wife even warned him not to do anything to Jesus because of a dream she had, according to Matthew 27:19: "While Pilate was sitting on the judge's seat, his wife sent him this message: 'Don't have anything to do with that innocent man, for I have suffered a great deal today in a dream because of him.'"

In the end, Pilate tried to absolve himself from any guilt in Jesus's death by washing his hands before the crowd. But he still delivered Jesus up to be crucified both to pacify the crowd, which had turned into a ranting mob, and to avoid a bad "performance review" with his superiors. He knew what was right—releasing Jesus—but he was too afraid to do it.

Not long after those events, the Romans removed him from office. He went back to Rome in disgrace and ultimately committed suicide.

SHE COULDN'T HELP IT?

On June 20, 2001, a mother committed a horrible act of child-murder. In a fit of deep depression and possible psychosis, she drowned each of her five children, ranging in age from a few months to seven years. She told police investigators that she did this because she was not "a good mother" and the children "weren't developing correctly."

In the ensuing trial, the jury learned that this woman suffered from deep post-partum depression (depression that follows the birth of a baby), had been on and off antidepressant and antipsychotic drugs, and had even been hospitalized in a psychiatric ward. Her husband turned out to be a passive father who probably did not help his wife in her serious condition.

What does the Bible say about such cases? Do we as Bible believers feel sorry for such people? Do we demand capital punishment, or do we call for mercy in the name of a compassionate God who cares about all his children, even those who have gone far astray?

What we're really asking is this: in God's justice, is there any room for extenuating circumstances, conditions that could have led an otherwise decent person to commit horrible acts?

Human courts strive for impartiality, but they are often blind to many of the real facts of a case, relying on faulty eyewitness accounts and forensic practices. In this world, while we might gain a measure of justice, in many other cases, because the court has not heard the "full story," there is gross failure and injustice.

The Bible teaches over and over that God is always just and fair in his judgments. Revelation 19:2 repeats a refrain found throughout Scripture: "for true and just are his judgments." Deuteronomy 32:4 tells, "He is the Rock, his works are perfect, and all his ways are just. A faithful God who does no wrong, upright and just is he."

God knows all the thoughts, motives, and inner workings of the person standing before him for judgment.

"O LORD, you have searched me and you know me. You know when I sit and when I rise; you perceive my thoughts from afar. You discern my going out and my lying down; you are familiar with all my ways. Before a word is on my tongue you know it completely, O LORD. You hem me in—behind and before; you have laid your hand upon me" (Psalm 139:1–5).

God's justice is unfailing, which means he cannot make mistakes. No innocent people will be sentenced with the guilty. "The LORD . . . does no wrong. Morning by morning he dispenses his justice, and every new day he does not fail" (Zephaniah 3:5).

God also cannot be "outjudged." In American justice, an appeals system can overturn one judgment after another. But God's judgments cannot be overturned; they always mete out absolute justice.

Jeremiah 32:19 adds, "Your eyes are open to all the ways of men; you reward everyone according to his conduct and as his deeds deserve."

God knows every person intricately. His judgments will be based on that absolute knowledge, not on the faulty evidence of eyewitnesses, the decrees of potentially erring psychologists, or the arguments of savvy lawyers. Ultimately, the Bible teaches that God is the final and perfect judge. No matter what crimes a person has committed, if he repents and asks forgiveness, he will find God to be merciful, full of grace and compassion.

Though some criminals have their day in human court, the real case, according to the Bible, has not yet been heard. God will dispense perfect and complete justice for everyone, justice the whole world will agree with and will even applaud.

If you are bothered by the way our courts sometimes dispense justice, you can take heart. God promises to bring full justice for every person in human history when his final judgment occurs. Everything will be considered—hurts, abuses, crimes done, and every other possible reason a flawed person may have done something wrong. As always, our hope is not in this world, but in God.

THE FANTASTIC VOYAGE

A boy, when asked what his Sunday school taught that day at church, said, "It was a story about a guy in the Bible named Moses. He led all these people to the edge of this sea. Then he had them build pontoon boats to use for a bridge to get them across. But the enemy's army came after them, so he had his people rig explosives under the bridge. After all the people got across, the enemies tried it too. But when they got out on the middle of the pontoon bridge, Moses signaled to his demolition people, and they blew the bridge to smithereens. All the enemies died instantly, and the people escaped."

The father, quite amazed, said, "The teacher told you that's what Moses did?"

The boy shook his head. "Not really. But if I told what the teacher said really happened, you would never believe it!"

HOW GOD GOT HIS THOUGHTS TO THE WRITERS OF THE BIBLE (5)

The true process of getting the Bible to us started with revelation. What is that, and how does it work?

Revelation shows us how God provided information about things we could never know without his help or intervention. What kinds of things? Events and truths the world argues about every day, like

- how we got here

- who God is and what he is like

- what happens when we die

- what God wants from us

- where the world is going

- how we can receive salvation and eternal life

- what really matters in life

- how God can make our lives fulfilling, beautiful, and holy

These are all issues we can't know about simply by our own investigation or research. Philosophers have wrangled with these questions for centuries. They've come up with a multitude of ideas and theories, from Nietzsche's "Superman" to Richard Bach's *Jonathan Livingston Seagull*. But all these offer little more than human answers to tough questions. You can take them or leave them.

Scientists might think they've unraveled the secrets of the universe with the mapping of DNA or the discovery of King Tut's tomb, but those things are merely discoveries of what was already there. God wants us to study his world and learn about it and him through it. But we need to ask, Where did the DNA come from? Who designed such a magnificent thing?

That's where revelation comes in. If God doesn't tell someone the truth about things we don't know and can't know, like how the world began and where it's all headed, and that person doesn't pass it on in an authoritative and trustworthy way, we have little hope of finding such answers. We may think humankind appeared here through the Big Bang and the process of evolution. But who saw those things happen? And if they did, who made them happen so that we ended up with Earth, the human race, and everything else? Science simply cannot answer those questions.

In fact, no one can. Except God.

Long ago, he decided to tell certain chosen people all about how we got here, who he is, what he desires, and so on. He chose one man, Abraham, to be the first in a long line of people he would use to tell the world about himself. Those people are the Jews. They're called the "chosen people" because God personally selected them for this task. They often revealed what he told them in stark, plain terms. In the Old Testament alone, you will find verses that say, "The Lord said . . ." and "God spoke . . ." and other expressions to indicate the words were from the very mind of God. The Jews weren't kidding. They believed their Scriptures were God's very words, without error, without evil infiltration, without any human embellishment or exaggeration.

(See the final installment of this article on page 118.)

THE STATIONS OF THE CROSS

There are fourteen incidents or "pictures" used to depict Jesus's route to the Cross in Catholic tradition. Many Roman Catholics pray at each station, using the rosary or other church-sanctioned methods, to gain grace or forgiveness from God. Regardless of the spiritual tradition, the actual stations (some of which are not found in the Bible) are:

1. Pilate condemns Jesus to death.

2. Christ carries the cross.

3. Christ falls to the ground under the weight of the cross.

4. Christ meets his mother, Mary, en route to Calvary.

5. Simon of Cyrene takes up Jesus's cross.

6. Christ's face wiped by St. Veronica (see The Face behind the Veil).

7. Christ falls a second time.

8. Christ tells the women of Jerusalem to stop weeping for him.

9. Christ falls a third time.

10. Christ stripped of his clothing.

11. Christ is nailed to the cross.

12. Christ is dying on the cross.

13. Christ's body is taken down from the cross.

14. Christ's body is placed in the tomb.

You can find pictures of these fourteen scenes along the walls of Anglican and Roman Catholic churches. During Lent believers often pray at each station and relive the story. This rite was instituted by the Franciscan monks. The actual service was not established, though, until the nineteenth century.

INVOKING CITIZENSHIP

There are two situations in the book of Acts where Paul used his Roman citizenship to escape various circumstances. In Acts 16:35–40, after being whipped and jailed in Philippi, Paul told the Romans involved in the punishments that he was a Roman. This sent them into a frenzy, because to carry out such punishments against a Roman citizen without a trial before Rome-appointed judges was seriously penalized. Such perpetrators could be executed. Thus, the local police begged Paul to leave quietly. He immediately told them they should appeal to him face-to-face. This they did, and Paul left the city without taking revenge.

The second case occurred after Paul was jailed in Jerusalem, where the leading Jews accused him of bringing Gentiles into the temple. When the commander of the Roman cohort apprehended Paul, he was about to have the apostle whipped, but Paul immediately told him he was a Roman citizen (see Acts 22:22–29). Immediately they released him. The next day Paul stood before the Jewish council, the Sanhedrin, and defended himself. This led to the Romans' sending him off to Caesarea because they heard of a plot to murder him.

Over the next few months, Paul gave his testimony to various Roman leaders— Felix and then Festus—but when they made no ruling about his guilt or innocence, he appealed to Caesar (see Acts 25). All Roman citizens had this right, and it literally meant the person invoking it would stand before Caesar himself. This resulted in the authorities' sending Paul to Rome, where the book of Acts leaves him at the end of the final chapter.

CHAPTER AND VERSE

Jews arranged their own system of chapters and verses, and it's not identical to the one you find in Bibles today. Stephen Langdon, Archbishop of Canterbury, divided the Old Testament into the chapters and verses we use today. He died in 1228.

HOW MANY? (OLD TESTAMENT)

The number depends on which translation of the Bible you pick. However, the English Old Testament King James Version was statistically tabulated by Dr. Thomas Hartwell Horne. Born in London, England, in 1780, he was educated at Christ's Hospital School and became a lawyer's clerk. He published his first book at the age of twenty, going on to pen many others. But his great work was the "Introduction to the Study of the Scriptures." This included the statistics we use today about the King James Version of the Bible. They are, for the Old Testament:

Books: 39

Chapters: 929

Verses: 23,214

Words: 593,493

Letters: 2,728,100

Middle verse of entire Bible: Psalm 118:8

Longest verse of the Bible: Esther 9:8

Shortest verse of the Bible: John 11:35 ("Jesus wept.")

Longest chapter: Psalm 119

Shortest chapter: Psalm 117

Occurrences of the word *and*: 46,277

Occurrences of the word *Lord*: 1855[5]

GOOD TO GREAT

Jesus was called a shepherd in several passages of the New Testament:

JOHN 10:11: *"I am the good shepherd. The good shepherd lays down his life for the sheep."*

HEBREWS 13:20: *"May the God of peace, who through the blood of the eternal covenant brought back from the dead our Lord Jesus, that great Shepherd of the sheep."*

1 PETER 5:4: *"When the Chief Shepherd appears, you will receive the crown of glory that will never fade away."*

These three adjectives—good, great, and chief—reveal three elements of Jesus's "shepherdness." Good: he is righteous and a worthy sacrifice for sins. Great: he is majestic and worthy of worship. And Chief: he is the first and foremost, deserving our loyalty, obedience, and love.

MOSES: MILQUETOAST TO MOVER OF MILLIONS

God can change a person from coward to courageous warrior. He can make men of milquetoasts, and lions of lambs.

Moses grew up in Pharaoh's palace, the adopted Hebrew son of Pharaoh's daughter. At the age of forty, he began to notice the plight of the enslaved Hebrews and considered ways of freeing them. One day, finding an Egyptian taskmaster beating a slave, Moses killed the taskmaster. When the murder became known, Moses fled Egypt into the desert. There he met Jethro, a believer in God, and served him the next forty years as a shepherd, perhaps because it was easy and Moses could just "disappear." Moses probably pummeled himself daily about his stupidity in killing the Egyptian taskmaster and having to flee from Egypt. A deep sense of inferiority and failure dogged him. We see this in the conversation he had with God at the burning bush.

God came to Moses through this bush on the mountain (see Exodus 2–3), telling him to go back to Egypt and free God's people from their slavery. Moses protested, squirmed, gave excuses, and finally just asked God to find someone else. He had no confidence he could do this job at all. God finally "ordered" Moses to get moving, and he did, probably feeling put upon and coerced. Over the next few months, though, things happened. Moses witnessed God's many miracles and plagues, such as water turned to blood, massive inundations of frogs, gnats, flies, and so on, and a "darkness that could be felt." God sent these upon the Egyptians because Pharaoh refused to set them free. At first, Moses flinched and fumed and threatened to quit (see Exodus 5:22–23). But day after day, Moses communed with God, learning more about his power and love. In the process, he grew in courage and confidence. By the time the tenth plagued occurred, Moses knew this God he served could do anything he chose to do. He was powerful, awesome, and totally trustworthy.

But the biggest test was coming. What would Moses do with an immediate threat?

We see the answer when God led Israel to the Red Sea. Pharaoh stormed after them in his chariots, and for a moment it looked like all was lost. Some screamed to simply cave in and go back to Egypt. Others shrieked, "Get rid of this Moses—he wants us all to die!" But Moses was a different man. He was no longer the milquetoast that argued with God at the burning bush. No, now he brimmed with courage and confidence. He jumped up onto a rock by the Red Sea and shouted, "Stand firm and see the salvation of God!"

What did Moses expect? He didn't know. God had not informed him. Moses was running on guts and glory. He had nothing more than simple faith that God would not let them die but would do something amazing.

At that moment, God spoke to Moses: "What are you waiting for? Let's get going! Hold your staff out over the sea."

Moses obeyed, and God sent a wind that drove the sea back and created a clear, dry path in the middle of it. The people crossed it safely. When the Egyptians attempted it afterward, though, Moses again stretched out his hand over the water, and God closed the sea over them, drowning them.

Where did this new, exciting, confident, and leading Moses come from? Straight from God's course in confidence and courage. Over those long years, God had trained Moses to believe God was with him and could do anything through him. Moses often did not know what God would do. But he stuck his neck out and obeyed what God told him. He learned true faith—proceeding with the conviction that God will do something Moses hadn't planned for or imagined.

SHROUDED IN MYSTERY

The sheet covering Jesus in his tomb was, according to Scripture, lying on a slab of rock when Peter and John arrived there on Sunday morning. Before them, several of the women had already gone there and reported that Jesus's body was gone. In John 20:6–7, we find the words, "Then Simon Peter, who was behind him, arrived and went into the tomb. He saw the strips of linen lying there, as well as the burial cloth that had been around Jesus' head. The cloth was folded up by itself, separate from the linen."

Normally, people who prepared a body for burial in a tomb like this wrapped the dead body in cloths and placed spices and myrrh in the folds to mitigate the odor emanating from a decaying body. In this case, Peter and John found those wrappings lying in the hewn niche where Jesus's body had been placed. The biblical text does not say they looked as if they had been unwrapped. Rather, the idea is that Jesus's body "passed through" the linen wrappings, leaving them in place like a butterfly does in leaving a cocoon.

The head wrappings, however, lay "separate from the linen," neatly folded up. What had happened? Perhaps Jesus, after rising from the dead through the other cloths, had folded up this part himself.

Today, many people believe we actually possess the shroud Jesus was buried in. It is called the Shroud of Turin and rests in Turin's Cathedral of St. John the Baptist in Italy.

TRANSLATION TIME[6]

The Bible has been translated into more languages than any other book. As of 2005, some 6,900 known languages exist in the world. Of these, 680 are in Africa, 420 in Oceania, 420 in Latin America and the Caribbean, 590 in Asia, 210 in Europe, and 75 in North America. At least one book of the Bible has been translated into 2,400 of those languages. The United Bible Societies presently work in more than six hundred other translation projects that are expected to soon have a Bible translation of at least one book, usually many more. At this time, more than 98 percent of the world's population has a part of the Bible written in a language they speak.

The last year for which statistics were available, the year 2000, revealed that more than 633 million books, booklets, and complete versions of the Bible were published. Taking that statistic back year by year, you find that literally billions of copies of the Bible have been distributed throughout the world since printing became available on a large scale in the late 1400s.

WHY SO MANY TRANSLATIONS?

It all goes back to Jesus's final statement to his disciples, known as the Great Commission. There are different versions in each of the gospels, and even another in Acts

1, but the most widely used statement is from Matthew 28:19–20: "Go and make disciples of all nations, baptizing them in the name of the Father and of the Son and of the Holy Spirit, and teaching them to obey everything I have commanded you. And surely I am with you always, to the very end of the age."

On this command, every missionary, translator, priest, preacher, leader, pastor, and minister has based his purpose in life. That purpose is to tell the story of Jesus, what he came to do (die for the sins of the world), how he lived (a perfect life), and how he rose again from the dead. A big part of telling that story is translating it into the language of the people the "preacher" is trying to reach. Many mission organizations today specifically train their missionaries to translate the Bible into the language of the people among whom they work.

FALSE GODS OF THE OLD TESTAMENT

1. The golden calf (Exodus 32), which Aaron made because Moses was absent

2. Nanna, a moon god, which Abraham worshiped in Ur (Joshua 24:2)

3. Asherah, goddess of Tyre (Judges 6:24–32)

4. Dagon, farm and sea god of the Philistines, father of Baal (Judges 16:23–30)

5. Ashtoreth, goddess of Canaan (1 Samuel 7:3–4)

6. Molech, god of the Ammonites, who demanded human sacrifices (1 Kings 11:7)

7. Baal, Canaan's highest deity (1 Kings 18:17–40)

8. Rimmon, Syrian god worshiped by Naaman the leper (2 Kings 5:15–19)

9. Nisroch, Sennacherib's Assyrian god (2 Kings 19:37)

10. Nebo, Babylonian god who was said to be all wise (Isaiah 46:1)

11. Marduk, primary god of the Babylonians (Jeremiah 50:2)

12. Tammuz, husband of Ishtar, goddess of fertility (Ezekiel 8:14)

MY FUNNY VALENTINE

In her book *Smile Please*, Mildred Topp wrote of the day she and her sister decided to send a valentine supposedly from her widowed mother to a prominent judge who had shown marked interest in the woman. Mildred wanted to use a new word she'd heard in Sunday school. "I'm not sure what it means," she said to her sister, "but it's in the Bible, so it must be OK. Besides it was used about King Solomon, so it's bound to be romancy enough for a valentine."

They sent the judge a gaudy, lace-bedecked valentine that read,

"If you will be my valentine, I will be your concubine . . ."

THE WIT AND WISDOM OF JESUS

"Do to others what you would have them do to you" (Matthew 7:12).

"Blessed are the poor in spirit, for theirs is the kingdom of heaven," and the rest of the Beatitudes (Matthew 5:3–12).

"You are the salt of the earth" (Matthew 5:13).

"You are the light of the world" (Matthew 5:14).

"This, then, is how you should pray: 'Our Father in heaven, hallowed be your name, your kingdom come, your will be done on earth as it is in heaven. Give us today our daily bread. Forgive us our debts, as we also have forgiven our debtors. And lead us not into temptation, but deliver us from the evil one" (Matthew 6:9–13).

"Ask and it will be given to you; seek and you will find; knock and the door will be opened to you" (Matthew 7:7).

"Watch out for false prophets. They come to you in sheep's clothing, but inwardly they are ferocious wolves" (Matthew 7:15).

"I am sending you out like sheep among wolves. Therefore be as shrewd as snakes and as innocent as doves" (Matthew 10:16).

"Are not two sparrows sold for a penny? Yet not one of them will fall to the ground apart from the will of your Father" (Matthew 10:29).

"The Son of Man is Lord of the Sabbath" (Matthew 12:8).

"Every kingdom divided against itself will be ruined, and every city or household divided against itself will not stand" (Matthew 12:25).

"Go and make disciples of all nations, baptizing them in the name of the Father and of the Son and of the Holy Spirit, and teaching them to obey everything I have commanded you. And surely I am with you always, to the very end of the age" (Matthew 28:19–20).

"Give to Caesar what is Caesar's and to God what is God's" (Mark 12:17).

"Watch and pray so that you will not fall into temptation. The spirit is willing, but the body is weak" (Mark 14:38).

"If anyone would come after me, he must deny himself and take up his cross daily and follow me" (Luke 9:23).

"It is easier for a camel to go through the eye of a needle than for a rich man to enter the kingdom of God" (Luke 18:25).

"The Son of Man came to seek and to save what was lost" (Luke 19:10).

"Father, forgive them, for they do not know what they are doing" (Luke 23:34).

"You must be born again" (John 3:7).

"I am the bread of life. He who comes to me will never go hungry, and he who believes in me will never be thirsty" (John 6:35).

"If anyone is thirsty, let him come to me and drink" (John 7:37).

"I have come that they may have life, and have it to the full" (John 10:10).

"I am the good shepherd. The good shepherd lays down his life for the sheep" (John 10:11).

"I and the Father are one" (John 10:30).

"By this all men will know that you are my disciples, if you love one another" (John 13:35).

"I am the way and the truth and the life" (John 14:6).

"Greater love has no one than this, that he lay down his life for his friends" (John 15:13).

WHIPPED INTO SHAPE

The story of Jesus's whipping out the money changers from the temple is rather amazing, considering he did it alone and against the power of all the authorities. The even more amazing fact is that he did it twice, once at the beginning of his ministry and once at the end.

In John 2:12–17 we find this event:

[Jesus] went down to Capernaum with his mother and brothers and his disciples. There they stayed for a few days.

When it was almost time for the Jewish Passover, Jesus went up to Jerusalem. In the temple courts he found men selling cattle, sheep and doves, and others sitting at tables exchanging money. So he made a whip out of cords, and drove all from the temple area, both sheep and cattle; he scattered the coins of the money changers and overturned their tables. To those who sold doves he said, "Get these out of here! How dare you turn my Father's house into a market!"

His disciples remembered that it is written: "Zeal for your house will consume me."

Jesus took these actions shortly after his first miracle at Cana, where he turned water into wine. The incident undoubtedly turned the Sadducees against him, for they owned and managed most of the businesses in the temple at the time, which made them all extremely wealthy. Like any normal businessperson, they likely thought what was bad for business was bad for the world. And that was how they regarded Jesus.

Nonetheless, the first time around yielded no permanent change, so Jesus performed it a second time at the beginning of the last week of his life on earth. You find the story in Matthew 21:12–13: "Jesus entered the temple area and drove out all who were buying and selling there. He overturned the tables of the money-changers and the benches of those selling doves. 'It is written,' he said to them, ' "My house will be called a house of prayer," but you are making it a "den of robbers." '"

These events are the "bookends" of Jesus's ministry, as if through them he enclosed his teachings and miracles with these two cleansings, to show his real mission was to advance his Father's kingdom and defend his honor, not just to redeem humankind and offer them heaven.

HOW GOD GOT HIS THOUGHTS TO THE WRITERS OF THE BIBLE (6)

To get his first words to us, God selected a man whom he would use to write down the first major elements of the story. That person was Moses. Moses began at the beginning and wrote the first five books of the Bible, telling us things we could not know without God's help.

Think of it: How did Moses get the story of creation? How did Moses know about Adam and Eve? How did Moses learn about the Tower of Babel and Noah's Ark and Abraham, Isaac, and Jacob? He may have learned a bit of it through his parents' telling him what they knew, as Pharaoh's daughter raised him in Egypt's palace. Perhaps while in Egypt, Moses visited the libraries the Egyptians built and read some of the great traditions. But ultimately, the only way he could have known all those things—with accuracy and credibility, not a false clue anywhere—was from God.

What did God do with Moses? He told Moses about everything from Creation on until Moses's life and times. Moses listened, remembered, took notes, and eventually wrote it all down so we in the twenty-first century would also know.

How did God actually reveal these things to Moses? There are a number of means God used:

- a burning bush that did not burn up, but spoke

- signs, wonders, and miracles (the ten plagues on Egypt)

- direct conversation, face-to-face

- personal appearances of God (called "theophanies"—"visible God")

- God's writing on stone tablets (the Ten Commandments)

- other people God spoke to (Aaron and Miriam—Moses's brother and sister)

At other times, God communicated his truth to people as he raised up prophets like Isaiah, poets like David, and wise men like Solomon. These men wrote down God's ideas and thoughts to his people. Some of the ways God did this was through

- angels
- dreams and visions
- the spoken words of prophets and priests and poets and others
- Jesus

These were the media God worked in. These were his "tools." An artist might paint with oils or acrylics. A poet uses words, images, rhyme, and meter. An architect employs brick, mortar, steel, and rivets. God utilized angels, dreams and visions, prophets, and ultimately Jesus to provide a straightforward, factual, accurate, and absolutely truthful picture of himself that we know as the Old and New Testaments.

Does that sound farfetched?

On the contrary, it seems like a highly likely way God would do it. Why would God risk his thoughts and words being whispered and garbled telephone-game style through the ages? Why would he use a redactor who, relying on his own whimsy and ideas, mixed together a bunch of unrelated stories? Why wouldn't God want to get the facts down in a medium that could be accurately passed on? Why wouldn't God, if he is all-powerful and all-knowing and all-everything else, be able to make sure we got the facts, just the facts, without embellishment?

I believe that's how he transmitted information to people like Moses, Samuel, David, the Gospel writers, and others. By revelation. God showed them the facts by various authoritative means, and they inscribed them with pen and ink. It's for this reason that people the world over, over two billion of them, consider God's Word as the very words of God. That Word has influenced countless people through the ages. Perhaps Charles Colson, the one-time Watergate conspirator, now professing Christian and founder of Prison Fellowship, a ministry to men and women in prison, said it best: "Yearly, the Bible outsells every bestseller. More than six-hundred million copies were published last year alone. Portions have been translated into more than 2400 languages and even carried to the moon."[7]

That's powerful testimony. Who else could have done such a thing but the Almighty God?

ACROSS THE YEARS

"In the past God spoke to our forefathers through the prophets at many times and in various ways" (Hebrews 1:1).

The Bible is a compilation of the recorded writings of many people over many years to whom God revealed different things about himself, life, the world, and salvation.

Why not take a moment and humbly thank God for revealing to us in the Bible all he did? God appreciates such reverence, and a little word of thanks might make his day!

THE BIBLE TELLS ME SO

The most astonishing application about revelation is that God chose to get involved in the first place. He could have left us on our own—mystified, worried, scared—fighting it out for every break and bit of turf on planet earth. He might have said to himself, "People messed the whole thing up when they chose to go their own way, so I'll let them rot! They don't care about me; I won't care about them." Or God could have said, "I'll give them one chance" and then have written a message on the moon or in the sky or with the stars, saying, "Hey, I'm up here. Believe!" But how effective would that be? And how informative?

Instead, he chose to come down among us and tell us face-to-face all the things we needed to know and do to survive and get along and even succeed as people. He chose to get down in our shoes and help us when we have needs, encourage us when we're worried, and be near when we're scared. He wants to be part of our lives!

That's the marvel. The Creator of the universe, the all-wise, all-knowing, all-powerful Potentate wants to be personally connected to each of us.

Karl Barth, the great Swiss theologian who wrestled with all the great questions about the Bible and theology and even wrote many books about his findings, was once asked on a visit to the United States what his greatest thought was. He considered for a moment, then he said, quoting a famous Christian song, "Jesus loves me this I know, for the Bible tells me so."

You might ask, What has God revealed? To be sure, he has told us how we got here, where we're going, and what to do to inherit eternal life. He could actually have given us much more: how he invented DNA, where he dreamed up the goldfish and giraffe, how to cure cancer. But those are things he has chosen not to reveal.

Yet we find great, heartrending things in his Word. And the greatest of all is that he loves us, he wants to know us and us to know him, and he longs to make our lives on earth a joy to behold.

That's a God worth reading about, don't you think?

THAT OLD-TIME RELIGION

A fourth grader recited the books of the Old Testament: "Genesis, Exodus, Leviticus, Numbers, Astronomy . . ."

THE TEN OLD LAWS?

Are the Ten Commandments relevant for today?

COMMANDMENT	FOUND IN	REPEATED IN NEW TESTAMENT
1. Worship no other gods.	Exodus 20:3	Acts 14:15
2. Make no graven image.	Exodus 20:4	1 John 5:21
3. Don't take God's name in vain.	Exodus 20:7	James 5:12
4. Remember the Sabbath.	Exodus 20:8	Colossians 2:16 (negates it)
5. Obey parents.	Exodus 20:12	Ephesians 6:1
6. Do not murder.	Exodus 20:13	1 John 3:15
7. Do not commit adultery.	Exodus 20:14	1 Corinthians 6:9–10
8. Do not steal.	Exodus 20:15	Ephesians 4:28
9. Do not lie.	Exodus 20:16	Colossians 3:9–10
10. Do not covet.	Exodus 20:17	Ephesians 5:3

Only the fourth commandment is nullified in the New Testament. All others remain in force.

THE PROOF IS IN THE PAGES

Some critics have claimed various passages in the Old Testament commit errors. Let's look at a few.

The Book of Daniel

The critics said that in the book of Daniel, the prophet spoke of Belshazzar's being the last king of Babylon and that he was killed when Cyrus entered the city with his army. Daniel also said Belshazzar was the son of Nebuchadnezzar. However, history shows Nebuchadnezzar's son was Nabonidus, who was the last king of Babylon.

Archaeologists later discovered four clay cylinders about King Nabonidus in Ur of the Chaldeans of Babylon. The cylinders contained information about the building of the Temple of the Moon God. It also contained a prayer to that god for Nabonidus's son, Belshazzar. The diggers also found that Belshazzar and Nabonidus ruled jointly at a time while Nabonidus was out of the kingdom city. Another cylinder also said that Gobryas, who was a general in Cyrus's army, recorded that Belshazzar died the same day. Belshazzar's name was mentioned many times in the artifacts about various contracts and properties that he bought. Finally, it was discovered that the Jews often referred to someone as the "son of" someone else, even if in reality he had been the boy's grandfather, as in the case of Nebuchadnezzar and Belshazzar.

The Book of Luke

Critics claimed repeatedly that Luke made all kinds of errors in names, times, and places. In Luke's defense, F. F. Bruce, a professor at the University of Manchester, England, wrote in *The New Testament Documents: Are They Reliable?* that

> One of the most remarkable tokens of Luke's accuracy is his sure familiarity with the proper titles of all the notable persons who are mentioned in his pages. This was by no means such an easy feat in his days as it is in ours, when it is so simple to consult convenient books of reference. The accuracy of Luke's use of the various titles in the Roman Empire has been compared to the easy and confident way in which an Oxford man in ordinary conversation will refer to the heads of colleges by their proper titles—the Provost of Oriel, the Master of Billiol, the Rector of Exeter, the President of Magdalen, and so on. A non-Oxonian like the present writer never feels quite at home with the multiplicity of these titles.

As a result, when Luke referred to proconsul Sergio Paulus in Acts 13:7 when Paul and Barnabas visited Cyprus, he could easily have made a mistake. Cyprus was governed by an "imperial legate" until 22 B.C., when it became a senatorial province. In A.D. 47, though, Luke used the correct term, "proconsul," rather than "legate," a mistake he could easily have made.

In the same way, Achaia was a senatorial province from 27 B.C. to A.D. 15. From that time until A.D. 44, it was ruled by a legate. But when Paul visited Corinth in A.D. 51, Luke correctly referred to Gallio as the "proconsul of Achaia" in Acts 18:12. In fact, a plaque was found in Delphi that identified Gallio as that proconsul at exactly the time of Paul's visit. He was only proconsul for a short time too.

The Book of Exodus

In Exodus 5, Moses wrote that Pharaoh, because of Moses's demands to let the people go free, stopped giving the Jews straw to use in the making of clay bricks. They had to forage for it, and it became scarce. However, they still had to make their quotas to build the store cities of Raamses and Pithom. Sir Flinders Petrie discovered the cities of Pithom and Raamses and discovered an incredible thing: they were built with mortar— a method not used elsewhere in Egypt but mentioned in Exodus 1:14. And then he found something else: the bricks on the lower levels had straw, but on the higher levels, the bricks had little to no straw—an amazing confirmation of the biblical account.

A BIRTHDAY PARTY?

Birthdays are often celebrated today with parties. One might think this a modern thing foisted on us, like so many other traditions by marketers and entrepreneurs. However, in Genesis 40:20, the Bible says that Pharaoh commemorated his birthday by throwing a feast for all his servants. And in Matthew 14:6, King Herod, at his birthday, watched his stepdaughter Salome dance. He was so entranced that he ordered that she be given whatever she asked. She went to her mother, Herodias, who hated John the Baptist because he pointed out that her marriage to Herod was not lawful because Herod had taken her from his half-brother Philip by divorce. Herodias told her daughter to demand John the Baptist's head on a platter. John, then imprisoned, was quickly beheaded because Herod didn't want to be embarrassed before all his guests, even though he genuinely liked John.

Imagine that as your birthday present!

CAN YOU SAY TETRAGRAMMATON?

Jews who practiced the law believed strongly that the third commandment, "You shall not take the Lord's name in vain," was inviolate. As a result, they never spoke God's primary name, Yahweh, aloud. So when rabbis read from the texts of the Bible or other documents, they did not say the name Yahweh when they found it in a text, but instead they used another name, Adonai, which means "LORD."

Later, when the Masoretes, a skilled group dedicated to copying the Scriptures from A.D. 400 till the time of the printing press, happened on a passage that spelled out the name, YHWH (called the "tetragrammaton" or "four letters" of the Name), they substituted the vowels of Adonai, which in Hebrew would be E-O-A. Thus, the name was transliterated to YeHoWaH—"Jehovah"—in Hebrew pronunciation.

"I AM"

The Name of all names—Yahweh—the primary name of God that God revealed to Moses at the burning bush in Exodus 3. It means, "I AM WHO I AM." That may sound circular, but God was making an important statement about himself. He used the words to claim, "I am the one who exists above and beyond all others. I am the one who exists on his own; I am not dependent on any other." God never had a beginning and doesn't have an end, but has always ever and forever "been." While we need food, water, shelter, and sustenance, and so on to survive in this world, God does not need anything. He is self-existing, dependent on nothing for his sustenance and survival. No one can ever destroy, maim, eliminate, or change him.

WHO'S MARCHING IN?

Contrary to popular belief, the word *saint* in the Bible is not used only for special people designated by the church as having mystical powers or a supernatural relationship with God. In Roman Catholic tradition, a saint has to perform at least one proven miracle and also meet a number of other qualifications. However, in the Bible, this was not the meaning.

Saint is translated from a Greek word that means "sanctified one," or "holy one"—a person whom God selected and separated from the world community for his special service and use. You might think of it the way a rich man might hire an assistant who serves only him. In the same way, a saint is someone God has called to follow him in a committed and persevering way.

Thus, every person who trusts in faith in Christ as Savior and Lord is a saint. So, we find 1 Corinthians 1:1–2 (NASB) (and many other places), "Paul . . . To the church of God which is at Corinth, to those who have been sanctified in

Christ Jesus, saints by calling . . ." Though the Corinthians were known to be unruly, at times immoral, and certainly no great examples of Christian virtue (read chapters 4–6 in particular), Paul still considered them saints because God had taken them out of the power and authority of the world and the devil and made them part of his family.

HOW GOD ENABLED MEN TO WRITE HIS WORD (1)

We looked earlier at the process of revelation, how God revealed various truths to people like Moses. But how do we know Moses didn't jazz up the stories, or add his own opinion, or, worst of all, make the whole thing up?

This leads us to the second major process by which God gave us the Bible: inspiration.

Inspiration is the way God got the ideas, stories, events, and truths from his mind to the minds of the people who then wrote it all down in words we could understand. God used their research, experience, passion, and style so that through the Holy Spirit their words became his words, and his words their words—accurate, holy, and absolutely true.

How does that work? Did Moses and all the others slip into trances or become possessed or just get fired up and then begin composing? Is that what we mean by "inspired," biblically speaking?

We'll continue this story line in several more installments (see page 150 for the next).

BE INSPIRED

inspiration: 1a. a divine influence or action on a person believed to qualify him or her to receive and communicate sacred revelation; 1b. the action or power of moving the intellect or emotions; 2. the act of drawing in, specifically, the drawing of air into the lungs. (MERRIAM-WEBSTER'S 11TH COLLEGIATE DICTIONARY)

If God wanted his word to be inspiring in the sense of making us "feel something acute, powerful, and life-changing," perhaps instead of the Bible he might have given us romance novels, the latest from a political pundit, or a Christian self-help book. Moving people emotionally is an important component of life, but few of us could stand a steady diet of "God's Chicken Soup for the Soul" packaged as the Word of God. Inspiration involves much more than rousing pep talks or stories. Don't expect to be moved to tears every time you read the Bible. That's simply not what inspiration is all about. It simply means that God has put his stamp of "authority, accuracy, and approval" on his Word because the Spirit of God led and guided the writers to produce precisely what God desired, not what they may have thought or believed.

YOU READ IT HERE FIRST

The oldest prediction of Jesus's first coming shows up in a very interesting prophecy from God in Genesis 3:14–15. There, God curses the serpent, after the serpent tempted Adam and Eve and talked them into eating the forbidden fruit, which led to universal sin and death for the human race. God said, "Because you have done this, cursed are you above all the livestock and all the wild animals! You will crawl on your belly and you will eat dust all the days of your life. And I will put enmity between you and the woman, and between your offspring and hers; he will crush your head, and you will strike his heel."

This curse on the serpent (the animal) meant he would become a snake. Previously, it had been one of the Garden's most incredible creatures, perhaps with the power to talk. The second part of the curse came on Satan, who had possessed the serpent according to several other biblical passages. That curse had four elements:

1. God would put a unique kind of hatred and loathing between Satan and the woman (which could be a reason that women often act especially wary and afraid of snakes), and she would in effect have a strong hatred for all immoral and sinful behavior incited by the devil.

2. God would also start a war between the serpent's "offspring" and the woman's "offspring." It's notable that God refers to a "woman's" offspring and not a "man and woman's" offspring. Many take this to refer to Jesus's being born of the Virgin Mary, where no physical human father had a part. It also prophesies about the particular hatred that would exist between Satan and Jesus himself.

3. This "offspring," referring to Jesus, would "crush" through the serpent's head, which clearly indicates Satan would be destroyed by Christ.

4. The serpent would "strike" Jesus's heel. That is, he would inflict harm, but not kill him, perhaps indicating the crucifixion and Jesus's subsequent resurrection.

For many centuries, these words became a great source of hope to humankind. Through them, God showed he would vanquish humankind's great enemy, the devil, and also provide a Savior who would triumph over him and bring in redemption and salvation to those who were lost.

PRECISE EXECUTION

For centuries, the Jewish mode for executing criminals involved stoning the victim to death. The accused stood in the center of a ring of his jury/accusers, and they hurled large stones at him until he was dead.

In Roman times, crucifixion became the standard means of capital punishment, as exhibited by Jesus's death. Amazingly enough, the Bible provides a graphic description of how this happened, in Psalm 22, written by King David more than seven hundred years before the practice became reality. There we see a number of amazing connections to the Roman form of torture:

1. Verse 1: Jesus quoted the very first line, "My God, my God, why have you forsaken me?" as he hung on the cross, perhaps as a means to point those observing to that very psalm (Matthew 27:46).

2. Verse 2 speaks of the fact that Jesus hung on the cross both night and day. How was this possible if he was on the cross only from 9 a.m. to 3 p.m.? Because, though Jesus was crucified in daylight, from 12 to 3 p.m., darkness covered the land (Matthew 27:45).

3. Verses 6–8 (NASB) say he was a "reproach." That is, people watching insulted and scorned him (Matthew 27:39–44).

4. Verse 11 tells us there was "no one to help," which is exactly what happened to Jesus in those hours. No one moved to do anything to stop it.

5. Verse 12 tells us he was surrounded by "strong bulls of Bashan," unbelievers (Matthew 27:12–13).

6. Verses 14–15 (NASB) indicate his physical pains: "poured out like water"—sweating profusely and dying of thirst; "bones out of joint"—precisely what happens when hanging in that position; "heart like wax"—melting within in and feeling faint; "strength dried up"—all personal ability gone; "tongue cleaves to my jaws"—great thirst; "You lay me in the dust of death"—the Father himself was the one who would put Jesus to death, not the crucifixion itself.

7. Verse 16 prophesies that his hands and feet would be pierced, the very thing the Roman soldiers did to Jesus in nailing him to the cross (Matthew 27:35).

8. Verse 18 indicates the executioners would "divide [Jesus's] garments among them" and "cast lots" for his clothing, which is precisely what the Roman soldiers did (Matthew 27:35).

This prophecy is especially amazing when you consider that crucifixion had not even been invented when David wrote these words.

ISRAEL'S SPLIT

Why did Israel split into two countries—Israel, the northern kingdom, and Judah, the southern—under King Rehoboam?

King Solomon, because of all his building projects, levied a heavy tax and labor toll on Israel. When he died and Rehoboam, his son, inherited the throne, the northern tribes under the leadership of a man named Jeroboam came to the new king and wanted to know if he would enslave them like Solomon had. Rehoboam consulted with the old guard of elders and advisers. They immediately told him to lighten up and the people would follow him forever. But then he turned to the younger men who had become his friends while growing up. They told him to get even harder. Thus, Rehoboam said, in effect, to Jeroboam, "My pinky finger will be like Solomon's loins." In other words, "I'll be a million times worse than my father Solomon ever was." Jeroboam led the people in rebellion and took the whole northern kingdom with him.

Why did Rehoboam make such a stupid, ill-fated decision? You can read about it in 1 Kings 11:11. There, because Solomon had turned to idols instead of God in his old age, God told him, "I will surely tear the kingdom from you, and will give it to your servant" (NASB). You can say all you want about Rehoboam being an idiot, listening to bad advice, and trying to be tough. But in the end, the reason he ended up with half of Israel under his leadership was because God had stripped the kingdom away from his father, Solomon.

JESUS'S SHOCKING BEHAVIOR

While the portrait of Jesus in the Gospels is mostly as a caring, compassionate shepherd to his errant sheep, there are some things that seem a little strange:

Jesus Refused to Tell Unbelievers He Was the Son of God

When Jesus revealed to his disciples that he was the Son of God, he repeatedly told them not to give this information out. Part of the reason was probably because the high priests and Sadducees needed some legal issue to use to arrest him. If he proclaimed himself the Son of God from the beginning, they could have thrown him in prison and sought execution through the Romans immediately for blasphemy. Thus, Jesus, because he needed to train his disciples and arouse the populace to his cause and truth, held off on that declaration until the very end. However, when the Sanhedrin finally confronted him about who he claimed to be, Jesus spoke clearly in Mark 14:61–62. There, the high priest asked Jesus, "Are you the Christ, the Son of the Blessed One?" Jesus immediately answered, "I am," then paraphrased Psalm 110:1, considered a tremendous prophecy of the coming of the Hebrew Messiah. What was the high priest's response? "Tearing his clothes, the high priest said, . . . 'You have heard the blasphemy; how does it seem to you?'" (Mark 14:63–64).

When there was nothing left to lose with these unbelievers, Jesus spoke plainly so they couldn't mistake him. As a result, they crucified Jesus because of this issue alone: because he claimed to be God incarnate, the Son of God, the Messiah.

Jesus Never Fought His Crucifixion; He Went Peaceably

Jesus's clear purpose in coming into the world was to accomplish redemption, the salvation of humankind. He came to pay the penalty for the sins of the world. He told his disciples about this many times, but perhaps the best statement came from his precursor, John the Baptist, who pointed Jesus out at the beginning and said, "Behold the Lamb of God who takes away the sin of the world." This was Jesus's mission from the beginning, not just to offer amazing teachings, perform miracles, even rise from the dead. No, his first and most important mission was to die, and thus, at the end, he didn't resist.

Jesus's death accomplished something never seen before, according to the Bible: the eternal salvation of humankind. As Peter wrote, "He Himself bore our sins in His body on the cross, so that we might die to sin and live to righteousness, for by His wounds you were healed" (1 Peter 2:24 NASB).

Where is Jesus now? Scripture says that Jesus is at the right hand of God where he prays and intercedes for his people at all times (see Acts 2:32–35; Hebrews 9:24, 7:25).

CAPITAL PUNISHMENT, OLD TESTAMENT STYLE

What crimes won the death penalty in the Old Testament?

1. Murder (Genesis 9:6; Exodus 21:22–23)

2. Kidnapping (Exodus 21:16)

3. Beating or cursing parents (Exodus 21:15)

4. Practicing magic or divination (Exodus 22:18)

5. Sex with animals (Exodus 22:19)

6. Worshiping false gods (Exodus 22:20)

7. Violating the Sabbath (Exodus 35:2)

8. Sacrificing humans to a god (Leviticus 20:2)

9. Committing adultery (Leviticus 20:10–21)

10. Committing incest (Leviticus 20:11, 12, 14)

11. Practicing homosexuality (Leviticus 20:13)

12. Blasphemy (Leviticus 24:11–14)

13. Making false predictions (Deuteronomy 13:1–10)

14. Repeated rebellion (Deuteronomy 17:12)

15. Premarital sex (Deuteronomy 22:20–21)

16. Rape of a virgin about to be married (Deuteronomy 22:23–27)

In contrast, there are no specific verses in the New Testament that call for the death penalty. Only the government was allowed to carry out capital punishment (see Romans 13), and they did so to punish evildoers, to protect the people from future crimes, and to warn them against committing the same crimes themselves.

LISTEN AND LEARN

Disciple means "learner." A rabbi in Jesus's day often led and taught several disciples who followed him and studied at his feet. Jesus called twelve men who were to be "with him." However, these were not the only disciples; many others followed Jesus but did not stay with him 24/7. For instance, we know he sent out seventy-two disciples at one point to do evangelism (see Luke 10:1). In John 6:66, the apostle John wrote that many of the disciples left Jesus because of some hard teachings. We also know that a number of women followed Jesus, including Mary and Martha (see John 11), Mary Magdalene, Cleopas, Salome, and Jesus's mother, Mary.

THE FIRST MISSIONARIES

Apostle means "missionary," "sent one," or "one sent out." The eleven disciples who continued following Jesus after his death and resurrection became apostles and missionaries at that point. Jesus ordered them to go throughout the world and spread the news of the gospel (see Matthew 28:18–20; Acts 1:8). Other apostles appeared later—Paul, Barnabas, Stephen, John Mark, Luke, and others. Jesus actually named the twelve disciples to be apostles in Matthew 10:1–4, but their final work as missionaries didn't start until after the Holy Spirit came upon them in Acts 2.

SPECTACULAR IN WHITE

Three disciples, Peter, James, and John, accompanied Jesus up on an unnamed mountain in Matthew 17:1–8. There they watched as Jesus was "transfigured" before them. The word could be translated "changed in appearance." Matthew says that Jesus's face "shone like the sun" and that his clothing "became as white as the light." While Jesus stood there on the mountain alone like this, two long-dead prophets, Moses and Elijah, arrived and stood with him. Why those two? Perhaps because they represented the two primary periods in miraculous Hebrew history. Miracles on a large scale were performed only two other times in Jewish history: under Moses (see the books of Exodus through Deuteronomy) and under Elijah and Elisha (see 1 Kings 17–2 Kings 13). Jesus's life and times and the following period under the apostles are the only other periods where specific people had the power to perform miracles at will.

These two men also appeared on the mountain to the disciples as bright as the sun and beautiful. Why did this happen? It was a picture of Jesus's glory, what he (and those who follow him) would look like in the future kingdom of God. Through this, Jesus convinced the disciples he truly was the Son of God. As the disciples watched, a shining cloud appeared over them and a voice from heaven spoke out of the cloud, saying, "This is my Son, whom I love; with him I am well pleased. Listen to him!" I suspect after this spectacle, those three disciples in particular paid much closer attention to everything Jesus said, don't you?

JOSHUA FIT THE BATTLE

When John Garstang excavated the ruins at Jericho from 1930–36, he discovered several amazing facts. First, he found that the walls fell outward instead of inward as you might expect during a siege. This parallels precisely what happened according to the biblical account (see Joshua 6:20), which says the "walls fell down flat" (NASB). This enabled the Israelite attackers to climb over it and attack the city.

Various people have attacked the Bible's integrity by saying that it was impossible for an army as large as Joshua's to march around a city that big seven times in one day. However, Garstang found that the city was actually smaller than the site occupied by a large metropolitan church, perhaps less than one hundred acres.

Finally, Garstang found the ruins filled with charcoal and the remains of a conflagration, which, according to Joshua 6:24, was precisely the result of what Israel did to the city. Garstang was convinced not only that he'd found the original Jericho the Bible speaks of, but that the Bible's history of the conquest was exactly as it happened.

WHO WERE THE HITTITES?

For many years, critics of the Bible claimed the writers made another mistake about the Hittites. These people are referred to throughout the Old Testament. However, no other records at the time proved their existence, so the critics said the Bible had to be wrong.

Nonetheless, Dr. Hugo Winckler, from 1906 to 1912, conducted excavations in Boğaskale, Turkey where he discovered thousands of tablets chronicling the history of a large Hittite empire that began in the fourteenth century B.C. In the process, Winckler found more than forty of their cities throughout the realm. Amazingly enough, the king of Egypt and the king of the Hittites worked out a treaty between the Egyptians and the Hittites. Many claimed the Bible had to be wrong about this too. However, on the palace wall of one of the excavated cities they found the whole treaty written out. Archaeologists have discovered that the Hittites ruled between Egypt and Babylon and were a tremendous superpower at the time.

NEW TESTAMENT WRITERS

According to tradition, and in many cases, actual references in the books themselves:

- Matthew the tax collector, one of Jesus's first called disciples, wrote Matthew.

- John Mark wrote the book of Mark, presumably with the help of Peter, one of Jesus's inner circle of three disciples (James, John, and Peter).

- Luke was not an apostle, but a Greek physician. He wrote the books of Luke and Acts.

- John, the son of Zebedee and brother of James, another of Jesus's primary disciples, wrote 1, 2, and 3 John, and Revelation.

- Paul wrote thirteen epistles, from Romans through Philemon. He was not selected by Jesus as one of the twelve original apostles, but was called later by Jesus on the Damascus road (see Acts 9).

- No one is sure who wrote Hebrews. Many have postulated that it was Paul, although the style in Hebrews is markedly different from his other writings. Others have said it might have been Apollos or another apostle.

- James, the half brother of Jesus, wrote James. He was not an apostle, but became a believer after Jesus's death.

- Peter wrote 1 and 2 Peter.

- Jude, the half brother of Jesus and brother of James, wrote Jude. He also was not an apostle but became a believer after Jesus's death and resurrection.

DOWN SOUTH—WAY DOWN SOUTH

Mr. Johnson, a businessman from Wisconsin, went on a business trip to Louisiana. He immediately sent an e-mail back home to his wife, Jennifer.

Unfortunately, he mistyped the address, and the e-mail ended up going to a Mrs. Joan Johnson, the widow of a recently deceased minister. The preacher's wife took one look at the e-mail and promptly fainted. When her family finally revived her and asked her what had happened, she nervously pointed to the message, which read, "Arrived safely, but it sure is hot down here."

MUTINY ON THE BOUNTY

The famous episode of the mutiny on H.M.S. *Bounty* in 1789 has been chronicled in books and movies. Not as well-known are the circumstances of the mutineers after they sent Captain Bligh on his way. Though some of the mutineers were later captured and executed, nine of them, including Fletcher Christian, the leader of the mutiny, settled on a distant island, later known as Pitcairn Island.

These men formed a colony and, with the natives they brought with them from Tahiti, they quickly descended into a debauched state of existence. After learning to make whiskey from a native plant, their ruin became obvious. Disease, immorality, and murder became rampant as different men claimed various wives of the others. In time, every one of the white men and male natives was dead except one, Alexander Smith. In time, he found a Bible among the things taken from the *Bounty*.

He began studying the Bible as he'd never read it before. In time, he decided to begin applying it to his life and the lives of those remaining. He taught classes to the women and children. They all believed in Christ and began to live completely different lives as a result.

Twenty years later, the island was discovered. There, the crew found a near-utopian community. The people lived in harmony and moral decency, prosperity and peace. There was no crime, disease, immorality, insanity, or illiteracy.

Smith gave all the glory to the Bible and its application.

IS THE NEW TESTAMENT FULL OF ERRORS?

While critics have said that the New Testament is full of errors, problems, and contradictions, the fact is that the actual text, the words and sentences, have been proven to be highly accurate insofar as copying and reproduction is concerned. No originals remain of the letters, Gospels, and so on found in the New Testament. However, through a process known as "textual criticism" in which scholars compare the copies we have of the New Testament with other copies, they have found some rather remarkable realities.

1. Of the approximate two hundred thousand words in the New Testament, only four hundred are questioned as to their meaning and definition from the originals.

2. Of those four hundred words, even if scholars can never determine what the original statements were, none of the great or even small doctrines or truths

of the New Testament would be in doubt. In other words, the text we use today is more accurate than any other writing from ancient history, including Homer's *Iliad*, Caesar's *Gallic Wars*, and all others.

3. Scholars are satisfied that today we use virtually the same books and words as read by those who first received the writings of the New Testament.

IT'S A MIRACLE!

A miracle involves any event, situation, or experience that goes against the natural order and laws of nature. It can only be explained by supernatural intervention. "Supernatural" means anything not natural. "Intervention" speaks of actions that can only be done on a divine scale. If someone places grape juice into a bottle and it ferments naturally, thus becoming wine, no one would be at all amazed. But if a person goes to the well, fills a jar with water from the well, returns to the house, and then Jesus tells him to taste it, and the water in the jug is now wine in the sense of fermented grape juice that can induce drunkenness if someone drinks too much, then that is a miracle.

If a person is blind, but he receives certain surgical implants or medications that enable him to see again, that is medicine. But if a man born blind asks Jesus to heal him so he can see, and Jesus says, "According to your faith will it be done to you" (Matthew 9:29), and the man suddenly sees, that is not a normal medical process; that is a miracle.

Miracles usually involve sudden, complete, unchangeable, and simple acts that lead to lifelong transformation. Natural events follow normal and natural processes. Thus, a miracle occurs when an outside force or person acts in the natural world and produces a supernatural result. The parting of the Red Sea, raising the dead man Lazarus, and God's sending lightning to ignite a sacrifice are all real miracles. When these things are written about by authentic eyewitnesses, their testimony is usually compelling and convincing. That as what you have in the Bible records.

MIRACLES HAPPENED

If you leave out the creation of the universe, Earth, and all its contents in six days (see Genesis 1–2), you find these other miracles in the Old Testament (listed in order of magnitude):

1. the ten plagues on Egypt that finally persuaded Pharaoh to let the enslaved Israelite people go under the leadership of Moses (Exodus 5–13)

2. the flood in the time of Noah that destroyed the whole earth except his family and the creatures he had secured in the ark (Genesis 6–9)

3. the parting of the Red Sea so Israel could pass through on dry land, but the water closed up on the Egyptian chariots as they tried to follow (Exodus 14)

4. the sun caused to "stand still" at the request of Joshua as he fought a battle where he needed more daylight to win (Joshua 10:12–14)

5. the summons by Elijah of God's lightning on Mount Carmel to burn up a sacrifice and prove he was the real and true God against Baal, the idol god of lightning and weather (1 Kings 18)

6. parting of the Jordan River to let Israel cross into the "land of milk and honey" under the leadership of Joshua (Joshua 3)

7. raising of the dead (three instances): the widow's son resuscitated by Elijah (1 Kings 17:17–24), the Shunammite's son raised by Elisha (2 Kings 4:8–37), and a man who died but came alive again after his body touched the bones of Elisha (2 Kings 13:21)

8. various healings: the miraculous healing of King Hezekiah, and God's causing a shadow to go backward ten steps (2 Kings 20:1–11); the miraculous healing of Naaman, a leper (2 Kings 5:1–19) by dunking himself in the Jordan River seven times; the miraculous afflicting and then healing of Miriam of leprosy because of her attack on her brother Moses (Numbers 12); the miraculous healings of people who were bitten by poisonous snakes and looked at the "bronze snake" in faith (Numbers 21:8–9)

9. various conquests and military victories: Amalek defeated (Exodus 17:8–13); destruction of Korah (Numbers 16:28–32); Jericho annihilated by the blowing of horns and a shout from Israel (Joshua 6:6–20); 120,000 Midianites destroyed by 300 Israelites under the leadership of Gideon (Judges

7:16–22); killing of the Philistines by Samson using the "jawbone of a donkey" (15:15) and at his death by pushing down the pillars of the temple of Dagon (Judges 16:30); and men killed by fire from heaven at Elijah's prayer (2 Kings 1:10–12)

10. various miracles in the book of Daniel, including the survival of Shadrach, Meshach, and Abednego in the furnace of fire (Daniel 3:1–25), the "writing on the wall" at Belshazzar's feast, prophesying his destruction (Daniel 5:1–30), and Daniel saved from the lions in the lions' den (Daniel 6:1–23)

11. various special miracles done for Israel in the time of Moses: Moses's rod turned to a serpent and back to a rod (Exodus 4:4–6); Moses's hand afflicted with leprosy and immediately healed (Exodus 4:6–7); sweetening of the bitter water (Exodus 15:25); water from the rock at Horeb (Exodus 17:6); water from a rock in Kadesh (Numbers 20:11)

COMMON MIRACLES

There were only a few periods in Jewish history when miracles were common:

The first happened during the time of Moses in which God afflicted Egypt with ten plagues that led to the Israelites' release. In the wilderness, God performed many other miracles, such as the parting of the Red Sea, the appearance of the cloud by day and the pillar of fire by night, the presence of the manna each morning, and various supernatural punishments, to name only a few.

The second period of miracles occurred under the prophetic ministries of Elijah and Elisha. Elijah prayed, and God halted rainfall for more than three years in Israel. We also see his confrontation on Mount Carmel, in which God sent a lightning bolt that consumed a sacrifice with its altar and the water in the moat around it. Elisha performed other miracles by raising a boy from the dead, making a metal ax head float, and saving people from poisoned food.

The third period of miracles happened during Jesus's ministry and then in the early-church years that followed.

WHEN JESUS SAID "FOLLOW"

Jesus told his followers to take up their cross and follow after him. He meant that anyone who wanted to follow had to be prepared to obey him to the point of death. In the Roman Empire, a person who carried a cross had been sentenced to death.

Jesus said many other things about a disciple's commitment to him. When he called the first disciples, he told them, "Come, follow me, . . . and I will make you fishers of men" (Mark 1:17). By these words, he gave them a great hope of personal significance and enduring legacy: they would lead others to salvation and eternal life. Jesus did not only promise them death and misfortune.

Perhaps Matthew 10:16–42 is Jesus's best outline of what it means to follow him. There he tells the disciples that he sends them out "like sheep among wolves." He assures them they'll be dragged as prisoners before governors and kings because of their commitment to him. The purpose? So they will speak the truth even to those august personages about Jesus. He went on to say that they would be scourged in the synagogues and hated by many. Regardless, he assured them there was no need to fear those who "kill the body, but cannot kill the soul." God would take them to heaven, and that alone makes every suffering worth it.

Perhaps Jesus's most incredible statement is found in Matthew 10:34: "Do not suppose that I have come to bring peace to the earth. I did not come to bring peace, but a sword." He told the disciples that sons and fathers, mothers and daughters, and others would disagree about Jesus and thus be at odds to the point that children would betray their parents. Yet, once again, Jesus said that their reward is protected and definite and that "anyone [who] gives even a cup of cold water" to a child "will certainly not lose his reward" (Matthew 10:42).

HOW GOD ENABLED MEN TO WRITE HIS WORD (2)

Many ideas about inspiration exist today. For instance, you're on a sports team, it's halftime, and the coach wants to crank up his players. He gives a rousing pep talk and even drags in a story about his crippled grandson Reggie and then he concludes, "Win this one for Reggie!"

Ever heard a story like that? Such speeches can inspire us in the sense that they touch our emotions and make us feel excited or revved or just mellow inside.

But that is not what biblical inspiration is all about.

Another way we look at inspiration involves something like a musical presentation—

an orchestra playing Beethoven, or a jazz quartet playing Ellington, or even a rock band belting out their latest hits. We get all hopped up, goofy, turned on, and even a little crazy! We might whoop or cry or laugh or dance.

But again, that is not what biblical inspiration is all about.

On another front, a book lover purchases an "inspirational romance" in the local Barnes & Noble. She can be sure that by the end of the story she will be crying her eyes out with joy and exhilaration over the success and triumph of two young lovers seeking true romantic bliss.

You might attend a church service, hear an "uplifting" sermon, and walk out feeling inspired to change your life.

Sitting at your computer, you might whip out a tremendous short story or poem for your best girl, even feeling carried along by some strange inner muse or force you can't explain.

We call such things inspiration.

But none of that is what biblical inspiration is all about.

All right, if that's what it's not, then what is it?

(See the next installment on page 161.)

NO PITCHFORK HERE

Though popular culture would have us believe Satan is a man dressed in a red suit and carrying a pitchfork (or trident), the Bible paints a very different picture of this enemy of God and God's children. *Satan* means "adversary" or "one who opposes." In that respect, Satan won his name by opposing God, the Creator of the heavens and the earth. Through such passages as Isaiah 14:12–14; Ezekiel 28:11–19; Matthew 4:1–11, and much of the book of Revelation, we learn that Satan was originally Lucifer ("shining one"), the highest archangel God ever created and the most magnificent. He is a person and was once the "covering cherub," literally an angel with four wings and four faces who protected the holiness of God. Because of pride and jealousy, Lucifer rebelled against God's rule and sought to set up his own kingdom, populated with a third of the angels of heaven who rebelled with him (see Revelation 12:4).

He was cast out of heaven and thrown down to earth, where today he and his cohorts tempt, accuse, deceive, fight, and devour men, women, and children. The apostle John said that the "whole world lies in the power of the evil one" (1 John 5:19 NASB), but Jesus assured us that we should not fear for "greater is He who is in [us] than he who is in the world" (1 John 4:4 NASB).

God presently allows Satan and his rebels to have limited but broad power in the world to tempt and test people. In some cases, God allows Satan to use great power over people (see Job 1 and 2). But Satan is always entirely under the rule of God and can do nothing unless God in his sovereignty permits it. Ultimately, Satan will be chained in hell forever (see Revelation 20). He will never again tempt or mislead peoples or nations, and the new universe will be marked by equity, justice, goodness, and righteousness.

GREAT PEOPLE TALK ABOUT THE GREATEST BOOK

C. S. Lewis: "No philosophical theory which I have yet come across is a radical improvement on the words of Genesis, that in the beginning God made the heaven and the earth."

Dwight Moody, evangelist of the nineteenth century: "In prayer we talk to God. In Bible study, God talks to us, and we had better let God do more of the talking."

"God did not give us the Scriptures to increase our knowledge, but to change our lives."

Joseph Cook, unknown: "Do you know a book that you are willing to put under your head for a pillow when you lie dying? That is the book you want to study while you are living. There is but one such book in the world. The Bible."

Charles Spurgeon, nineteenth-century British preacher: "A Bible which is falling apart usually belongs to someone who is not."

Martin Luther, German Protestant Reformer of the sixteenth century, about studying the Bible being much like gathering apples: "First, I shake the whole tree that the ripest might fall. Then I climb the tree and shake each limb, and then each branch and twig, and then I look under each leaf."

Time magazine, December 30, 1974, about the reliability of the Bible: "After more than two centuries of facing the heaviest scientific guns that could be brought to bear, the Bible has survived—and is perhaps the better for the siege. Even on the critics' own terms—historical fact—the Scriptures seem more acceptable now than they did when the rationalists began to attack."

Mark Twain, American humorist: "Most people are bothered by those passages of Scripture which they cannot understand; but as for me, I have always noticed that the passages in Scriptures which trouble me most are those which I do understand."

KNOCK, KNOCK

"I am the door; if anyone enters through Me, he will be saved, and will go in and out and find pasture" (Jesus, in John 10:9 NASB).

If you want to find the passageway to eternal life, joy in this life, and a sense of personal significance, the "way" is not a physical door, a gate, the opening of a cave (as in Plato), a signpost for a road, or anything like that. Rather, it is a person: Jesus. By believing in him, according to Jesus's own words, you will enter a world never before seen, and you will know for certain that you belong to him and can live without fear of death all your days.

HOW TO STUDY THE BIBLE

F. B. Meyer, early twentieth-century preacher and teacher: "Read the Bible not as a newspaper, but as a letter from home. If a promise lies upon the page as a blank check, cash it. If a prayer is recorded, appropriate it and launch it as a feathered arrow from the bow of your desire. If an example of holiness gleams before you, ask God to do as much for you."

SAFEPACK

When you read a passage of Scripture and think about it, use this acrostic:

S—Is there a **S**in to avoid?

A—Is there an **A**ttitude to change or adopt?

F—Is there a way to exercise my **F**aith?

E—Is there an **E**xample to follow?

P—Is there a **P**rayer to voice?

A—Is there an **A**ction to do?

C—Is there a **C**hallenge to take up and meet?

K—What is the **K**ey to growth in my life today?

KEEP READING[8]

Guinness World Records reveals how long it takes to read through the entire Bible. A pastor named Don Taggart of Pontoloc, Mississippi, enlisted the youth in his church in 1977 to read the Bible out loud straight through. It took fifty-two hours for the Old Testament, and fourteen hours for the New Testament.

IT TAKES MORE THAN A VILLAGE, COMRADE

In the village of Kalinovka, Russia, the priest of the church began a program of Bible memorization for the children. His prize pupil memorized all four of the Gospels— Matthew, Mark, Luke, and John—and was so good at it, he recited them nonstop and without error before the whole congregation, winning a special prize.

Sixty years later, this same person enjoyed reciting the Bible, but in a way that would have enraged the old priest. His name? Nikita Khrushchev of the Soviet Union, a communist nation built on the principles of atheism.

The point: anyone can know and recite the Bible. But how it has affected his life is what really matters. As James 1:22 (NASB) says, "Prove yourselves doers of the word, and not merely hearers who delude themselves." And later, James 2:19 (NASB): "You believe that God is one. You do well; the demons also believe, and shudder."

Bible: a collection of different legends, mutually contradictory and written at different times and full of historical errors, issued by churches as a "holy" book (*DICTIONARY OF FOREIGN WORDS,* SOVIET GOVERNMENT, 1951).

Voltaire, the French philosopher of the eighteenth century, said, "Fifty years from now the world will no more hear of the Bible."

Fifty years after Voltaire said this, the British Museum paid half a million dollars to the Russian government for a copy of the Bible. Voltaire's book sold in Paris for less than five cents. His printing shop was also bought and used to print—you guessed it—Bibles.

HALLELUJAH!

Messiah means "the anointed one" in Greek. "Christ" is the English transcription of the same Greek term—*cristos*—and also means "anointed one." Anointing was meant to show that a special gift of the Spirit and of grace for some important mission, ministry, or deed had been given to the person anointed. Lucifer was called the anointed cherub in Ezekiel 28. The prophet Samuel anointed teenaged David with oil to show he was God's choice to become the future king of Israel to replace the errant King Saul.

In Hebrew history, the specific name, the "anointed one," held a singular and significant place. The Messiah would establish peace for Israel. He would rule the nations of the world with a "rod of iron." He would also lead a future kingdom that would go on for a thousand years, and then into eternity, forever and ever. He would become the first truly righteous—good, just, and godly—king ever to rule on earth.

In the Old Testament, Isaiah pictured the Messiah as a "suffering servant" who would reconcile God's people to God the Father. Isaiah 53 relates his very special period of suffering, saying God himself would "smite" him, "afflict" him, and ultimately kill him in the place of sinners. Thus, the Old Testament pictures the Messiah in what many thought was a contradictory portrait: a just and righteous king ruling the world and a suffering servant who pays for the sins of the world by dying for it.

Many of the Jews of Jesus's day rejected this image, preferring the kingly, ruling, conquering elements rather than the suffering aspects. They rejected Jesus because not only wouldn't he bring in the kingdom they wanted to rule in as his subordinates, but because he was rough and unlearned and ran against all their ideas of a conquering hero.

When Jesus was crucified, he fulfilled his role as the suffering servant. He died for the sins of the world, redeemed humanity from its slavery to corruption and degradation, and reconciled all people to God. In the future, when he returns as the glorified, all-powerful conqueror, he will appear as the true king who will reign righteously, bring in justice for the afflicted and oppressed, heal every illness, establish world peace, and right every wrong.

Ultimately, the Messiah is the amazing prophesied person who will establish and ensure the kingdom of God in the new heavens and earth. He is our Lord, our Master, our King, our friend, our brother, and our Savior all in one—Jesus.

DINNER IS SERVED

What was served at the Last Supper of Jesus with his disciples?

Because it was Passover, we know exactly what was served: unleavened bread, bitter herbs, wine, and roast lamb. The disciples lay prone, propped up by pillows, around a low table. Using torn pieces of unleavened bread, they would dip into the roast lamb—broken up and cooked through—grab a chunk, and eat it on the bread.

Jesus, however, wanted to commemorate this Passover in a special way, as he meant to institute a whole new order and tradition for his followers. Thus, it's often called the "Last Supper"—Jesus's last meal with his followers until he returns to earth. At that supper he created a sacrament that included unleavened bread and wine. According to Paul (1 Corinthians 11:23–26), Jesus picked up a bit of bread and said, "This is my body, which is for you, do this in remembrance of me." He performed this rite at the beginning of the dinner. When all was finished, he picked up the cup of wine and said, "This cup is the new covenant in my blood; do this, whenever you drink it, in remembrance of me."

The Lord's Supper, as a result, is the most important "ordinance" of the Christian church. It is a remembrance of Christ's death for our sins. When Christians take it, they are to confess any sins and ask for forgiveness, because one cannot eat the Lord's Supper if he favors sin in his heart or life (see 1 Corinthians 11:27–34). To do so risks God's punishment. Apparently, in the Corinthian church some individuals were partaking in the Lord's Supper unworthily, and God had brought sickness and even death. It is an extremely serious rite that Christians are advised to take regularly and soberly.

The Roman Catholic Mass is centered on this event, which they call the Eucharist. The word means to "show favor or gratitude." Roman Catholic tradition holds that the bread and wine, once consecrated by the priest, actually in a mystical sense become the body and blood of Jesus Christ by a process called transubstantiation.

Martin Luther (1483–1546), who began the Protestant Reformation in 1517 and broke from the Roman Catholic Church, rejected this doctrine. He believed in something else called consubstantiation in which the presence of the Spirit of Jesus was "around, by, over, and under" the bread and wine but did not actually "become" his body and blood.

John Calvin (1509–1564), a French theologian, and Ulrich Zwingli (1484–1531) in Switzerland, both from the same period, came to different conclusions about the Lord's Supper, believing that it was a remembrance, a kind of object lesson Jesus used to remind his followers of what he had done for them.

The controversy about who is right still rages today.

PEACE AND JESUS

Jesus is often called the Prince of Peace. He made it clear in several passages that he came specifically to bring peace to the hearts of those who would believe. For instance, in John 14:27, he told his disciples, "Peace I leave with you; my peace I give you. I do not give to you as the world gives. Do not let your hearts be troubled and do not be afraid." In John 16:33, he assured them, "I have told you these things, so that in me you may have peace. In this world you will have trouble. But take heart! I have overcome the world." His birth was announced by angels who promised peace: "Glory to God in the highest, and on earth peace to men on whom his favor rests" (Luke 2:14).

However, Jesus also made it clear that in at least one sense he didn't come to bring peace, but a sword. He said in one of his messages to the disciples about their forays into the world to convert men and women to the truth of the gospel, "Do not suppose that I have come to bring peace to the earth. I did not come to bring peace, but a sword. For I have come to turn 'a man against his father, a daughter against her mother, a daughter-in-law against her mother-in-law—a man's enemies will be the members of his own household'" (Matthew 10:34–36).

Jesus plainly was predicting that his message would bring dissension and argument, and that believing in him could pit a son against a father, a daughter against her mother and so on. Obviously, this is exactly what happens today in many families. When a Jew turns to Christ, often his or her "unbelieving" relatives will hold a funeral service, "burying" the person they believe has defected. In Muslim and Hindu countries, conversion invites death.

HOW GOD ENABLED MEN TO WRITE HIS WORD (3)

In two previous installments, we looked at theories of inspiration that are not true. Here is the true one:

Second Timothy 3:16–17 reveals exactly how God took Moses and all those other writers of the Bible from revelation to inspiration. Those verses say, "All Scripture is God-breathed and is useful for teaching, rebuking, correcting and training in righteousness, so that the man of God may be thoroughly equipped for every good work."

This passage shows that the Bible elicits the very "breath of God." What do you do when you speak out loud? You exhale air over your vocal chords, and your lips, tongue, and mouth shape the air into sounds. Words are little more than human breath manipulated and sculpted into understandable sounds.

When the Bible says it is "God-breathed," it means the words have the very life and breath of God in them. As men wrote the Bible, God breathed or spoke those words through those men. The Spirit of God grasped their minds, research, thoughts, ideas, convictions, paper and pen and guided it all so that what came out was the precise word of God.

Another statement from Paul is helpful. He wrote in 1 Corinthians 2:10–13 that God "revealed them through the Spirit . . . that we might know the things freely given to us by God, which things we also speak, not in words taught by human wisdom, but in those taught by the Spirit, combining spiritual thoughts with spiritual words" (NASB).

Notice several elements of inspiration from this passage:

1. God revealed them through the Spirit. Here we're back to revelation, God showing the writers things they never knew or could know.

2. God did it through the Spirit. The Holy Spirit, the third person of the Trinity, on some level "spoke" into the minds and hearts of the writers.

3. These words weren't taught by human wisdom. They weren't the opinions of people, or made up by them.

4. They were taught by the Spirit. Presumably a process took place in which the Spirit of God literally "taught" the writers what to say on paper.

5. The Spirit combined spiritual thoughts with spiritual words. God didn't just communicate vague ideas to their minds, but actual "words" to the page.

But how did the communication happen?

(See the next installment on page 169.)

BUILDING THE PERFECT CHURCH

A rich man went to his pastor and said, "I want you and your wife to take a three-month trip to the Holy Land at my expense. When you come back, I'll have a surprise for you." The pastor accepted the offer, and he and his wife went off to the Middle East.

Three months later they returned home and were met by the wealthy parishioner, who told them while they were gone, he had had a new church built. "It's the finest building money can buy, Vicar," said the man, "No expense was spared." And he was right. It was a magnificent edifice both outside and in.

But there was one striking feature. There was only one pew, and it was at the very back.

"A church with only one pew?" asked the preacher.

"You just wait until Sunday." said the rich man.

When the time came for the Sunday service, the early arrivals entered the church, filed onto the one pew, and sat down. When the pew was full, a switch clicked silently, a circuit closed, the gears meshed, a belt moved, and, automatically, the rear pew began to move forward. When it reached the front of the church, it came to a stop. At the same time, another empty pew came up from below at the back, and more people sat down. And so it continued, pews filling and moving forward until finally the church was full, from front to back.

"Wonderful!" said the preacher. "Marvelous!"

The service began, and the pastor started to preach his sermon. He launched into his text and, when twelve o'clock came, he was still going strong with no end in sight. Suddenly a bell rang and a trap door in the floor behind the pulpit dropped open.

"Wonderful!" said the congregation. "Marvelous!"

GIANTS IN THE BIBLE[9]

1. Og, king of Bashan, who slept in a bed fourteen feet long and six feet wide (Deuteronomy 3:11)

2. Anak, the first in his race (Deuteronomy 9:2)

3. Sheshai, Ahiman, and Talmai, Anak's sons who were killed by Caleb (Joshua 15:14)

4. Goliath, a Philistine over nine feet tall, killed by David (1 Samuel 17)

5. Ishbi-Benob, a giant who was killed by Abishai, one of David's great men of war (2 Samuel 21:16)

6. Sippai, a Philistine giant slain by Israelite soldiers (1 Chronicles 20:4)

7. Lahmi, brother of Goliath, killed in battle (1 Chronicles 20:5)

8. Philistine giant who had twelve toes and twelve fingers, killed by David's nephew (1 Chronicles 20:6)

TO TELL THE TRUTH

Jesus prophesied in Matthew 24:5 that, "Many will come in my name, claiming, 'I am the Christ,' and will deceive many." In recent times, more people have made this declaration than perhaps at any other time in history. Some of the most famous people who have claimed to be God or Jesus or both are: Charles Manson, David Koresh, Jim Jones, Sun Myung Moon, Rasputin, Mahara Ji, Bhagwan, Herbert Armstrong, Adolf Hitler, Father Divine, and many others.

HEY, COUSIN!

According to Luke 1:36, Elizabeth, the barren wife of Zechariah, was a "relative" of the Virgin Mary. Elizabeth, miraculously pregnant by normal means with John the Baptist, was visited by Mary during her sixth month, and she gave Mary an amazing confirmation of God's Word and the angel Gabriel's visit where Mary was told she would bear the Son of God. This means that John the Baptist and Jesus were cousins. Does prophecy run in families? Rarely, as Jewish history shows, were prophets descended or related to one another. Even Elijah and Elisha were strangers. But this is one case where the Sovereign God brought two of the most famous men of history together by passion, belief, and blood.

FELIZ NAVIDAD

The first Christmas celebration resembling those we have today occurred on the shores of Haiti, when Christopher Columbus's ship the *Santa Maria* was wrecked off the coast. Columbus had been searching for gold along the coast of America. The sailors built a fort, La Natividad ("The Nativity") so they could be sheltered while Columbus rebuilt the ship, and they had a celebration, gifts, and feast on December 25.

THE DEAD SEA SCROLLS

Discovered in 1947 by an Arabic Bedouin while he was searching for his sheep among caves near the Dead Sea, these scrolls comprise the greatest find of modern history. The caves were located in the cliffs about a mile west of the northwestern corner of the Dead Sea, near a town known as Qumran. A large spring is nearby.

So far, eleven caves have been discovered in which various scrolls were hidden in large clay-fired jars and buried inside. One cave, number four, has yielded fragments from some 382 manuscripts, of which 100 are biblical Old Testament documents.

Some of the more famous finds are one complete scroll of Isaiah that is magnificent, to say the least. There is also a commentary on Habakkuk, which includes a complete copy of Habakkuk 1 and 2 in its text.

The people of Qumran lived there between 140 B.C. and A.D. 67. Most scholars believe the people there were Essenes, a small sect of Judaism, who were very conservative in outlook and had split off from the Hasidim (the forerunners of the Pharisees and who also exist as a sect today of very conservative Jewish believers). They were ascetics, devoted to the study of the Old Testament. There are no New Testament documents found among their hidden scrolls, mainly because the first New Testament epistles were penned around the same time that Qumran had run its course. However, there is much debate about whether John the Baptist had dealings with the sect, and also Jesus. There is no proof of either, but many scholars labor today to find a connection.

ABRAHAM'S GRAVE

Abraham purchased the cave of Machpelah from Ephron (see Genesis 23) and was buried there with Sarah (see Genesis 25:7–10) at the age of 175, "an old man and full of years." This means he had a great and blessed life that was filled with joyous and happy days. Today a mosque stands over the site, and entrance into the grave is forbidden. Isaac, Rebekah, Leah, and Jacob are also buried in it. It is presently in a field near Hebron, nineteen miles southwest of Jerusalem.

LOST MOUNTAIN

God gave Moses the Ten Commandments on Mount Sinai (see Exodus 19:20), also called Mount Horeb. The exact location is unclear, but many scholars believe it is Jebel Musa (Mountain of Moses) and Ras-Safsaf, a ridge with two peaks. One peak is

6,540 feet, and the other is 7,363 feet. At its base is the Monastery of St. Catherine's, which was built there specifically because the builders believed the mountain was the holy mountain of God.

THE ROAD TO JERICHO

Jericho is located five miles west of the Jordan and seven miles north of the Dead Sea, about eight hundred feet below sea level. It is sometimes called the city of palm trees because of the abundance of, well, palm trees. The Old Testament city was located about one mile northwest of the modern town on a mound called Tell el-Sultan, which has been much excavated by archaeologists.

SOLOMON'S TEMPLE

Solomon built his magnificent temple in Jerusalem on the site now occupied by the Dome of the Rock. Based on Ezekiel 40–48 and Revelation 11:1–2, many believers think the temple will be rebuilt in the "end times." Books have been written about plans in Israel and elsewhere to carry out the construction. The problem is that the Dome, one of Islam's most sacred sites from which Mohammed supposedly ascended to heaven, would have to be destroyed to make rebuilding possible. Such actions would undoubtedly infuriate the Muslim world, so some have suggested that an act of God, an earthquake, perhaps, might be the only way it could happen.

HOW GOD ENABLED MEN TO WRITE HIS WORD (4)

So how did God actually get his word from his mind to the pages on which his people were writing?

Theologians and Bible scholars have proposed several different ways God carried out this process.

Take a Letter

One was that he dictated the Scriptures to Moses, Joshua, Paul, and all the other writers of books of the Bible. They acted as little more than secretaries—God spoke; they wrote. They functioned as "personal assistants" taking their boss's dictation. No changes. No embellishments. No addition of their own words, no subtraction or even clarification. The boss said it; the assistant wrote it down. End of story.

Though this theory gained popularity for a long time with people such as theologian John Calvin (1509–1564) and others, it's now been discarded. One has only to read a few passages in the Bible to see that many different styles of writing occur. Instances include the writer offering his "opinion" (see 1 Corinthians 7:40). In what sense were such things "dictated"?

Danger, Will Robinson!

A second theory suggests that God somehow "possessed" the writers so they became like robots. They did precisely and only what he desired. In fact, they might not even have been conscious of what they were writing or how it happened. God took charge, his power grabbed their minds, and bang! Scripture resulted.

Again, this is an idea largely rejected by most conservative Bible scholars. Few writers indicate they experienced trances, became robotic, or were even "entirely possessed" by God in some way when they wrote. In fact, in a few cases, you find that conversations are quoted that are not in agreement with God's character or personality (see the book of Job for the arguments of Job's three friends). In other cases, we find people complaining to God about their circumstances, or arguing with God, or even trying to circumvent God's will. Would God take control of a person and then have him rail on about all the things wrong in his life? Many of the stories in the Bible read like a newspaper—a good reporter writing a news story. Why would someone have to slip into a trance or become a robot to do that?

"Becoming" the Word

A third line of reasoning proposes that God didn't really expect the writers of the Bible to get it all down accurately or precisely to begin with. He knew humans like to do things their way, and thus he let them write whatever they thought and felt and saw and experienced. If they messed it up, so be it. God would work around that.

Then, the theory continues, God takes those thoughts and ideas that were not necessarily his but could *become* his because they are in line with his thinking and invests those words with his power and presence. This is how it works: You might be reading along in the Bible, and suddenly that internal "still small voice speaks" to you out of the words on the page. It's at that moment that the words in the Bible, just the words of average people, nothing supernatural about them, actually become the Word of God! God takes mere human words and makes them his in that instance. God's "witness" to the words of men turns them into the very words of God.

This theory attracts many today, but it overlooks a number of problems. If this is the way God works, how is the Bible any different from any other book? Couldn't God "speak" through Shakespeare or Hemingway or Max Lucado just as effectively as through the Bible? Why would we even need a sacred book, if it's not really special or "truly from God" in any sense of the word?

Moreover, this disagrees with the testimony of many biblical writers, and even Jesus, who put Scripture on a much higher level. Jesus said in Matthew 5:18 (NASB): "For truly I say to you, until heaven and earth pass away, not the smallest letter or stroke shall pass from the Law until all is accomplished."

Jesus's Perception

From this quote of Jesus on the Sermon on the Mount, we see what a high opinion he had of Scripture. He said not the "smallest letter"—which was the Hebrew letter *yod* (it looks like our apostrophe)—would "pass away" or "be stricken from the record." Meaning, you couldn't overlook even the smallest letter when you were reading!

And then he took it even further. He said not a "stroke" would pass away. In Hebrew as in the English alphabet, many letters are determined by small lines added or subtracted from the way they're formed. For instance, an *n* is one letter, but add another leg and it becomes an *m*. A *P* needs only another loop to become a *B*. And an *I* only requires a little twist to become a *J*.

This is what Jesus meant by a "stroke." It's that small part of a letter that differentiates it from another. He was saying not even that can be overlooked, because God made his Word that perfect and accurate.

That's pretty astonishing, isn't it? It means God must have put some real care into the way his people wrote the Scriptures, because it will never pass away or be forgotten.

Typos! Typos! Typos!

Have you ever written something on a plain typewriter? If you're like me, what results is a document full of typos, grammatical errors, and plain lousy thinking. It takes many rewrites to get a piece of writing even close to right, let alone perfect. Even with modern spell-checkers and grammar-checkers, mistakes still slink through.

But Jesus said God didn't make one typo when he led a writer to pen his Word.

But what is the truth about this? How did God do it?

(See the next installment for this story on page 196.)

A MATTER OF OPINION

Found in a church bulletin referring to the pastor's illness:

GOD IS GOOD!
Dr. Hargreaves is better.

A KING IN THREE LANGUAGES

Pontius Pilate ordered that a sign be attached to the top of Jesus's cross. According to John 19:19–20, "Pilate had a notice prepared and fastened to the cross. It read: JESUS OF NAZARETH, THE KING OF THE JEWS. Many of the Jews read this sign, for the place where Jesus was crucified was near the city, and the sign was written in Aramaic, Latin and Greek." This enraged the leading Jews who had engineered the whole spectacle, and they stormed back to Pilate and demanded he retract the whole statement and replace it with something else. "The chief priests of the Jews protested to Pilate, 'Do not write "The King of the Jews," but that this man claimed to be king of the Jews.' Pilate answered, 'What I have written, I have written'" (John 19:21–22).

Was Pilate being "led" by God to play a part in his plan to exalt Jesus even in his death? Would God use an unbeliever like that to carry out his will?

The Spirit of God has done precisely that in other situations. For instance, John 11:49–52 says, "Then one of them, named Caiaphas, who was high priest that year, spoke up, 'You know nothing at all! You do not realize that it is better for you that one man die for the people than that the whole nation perish.' He did not say this on his own, but as high priest that year he prophesied that Jesus would die for the Jewish nation, and not only for that nation but also for the scattered children of God, to bring them together and make them one." Several other instances in Scripture show unbelievers speaking for God without intending to (see Balaam in Numbers 22–24, and Peter's words in Acts 4:27–28).

THERE'S NO EXCUSE FOR THAT!

Here's a list of excuses people in the Bible made for evil behavior.

1. Adam, when confronted about his sin of eating the forbidden fruit, immediately blamed it on Eve, "whom You [God] gave me" (Genesis 3:12 NASB).

2. Eve, in turn, blamed the serpent (Genesis 3:13).

3. Lot attempted to remain in Sodom when warned by angels of its impending doom, claiming he'd be killed on his way to the mountains by the destruction (Genesis 19:19).

4. Moses repeatedly offered excuses—he wasn't important enough or eloquent enough—for why he couldn't go back to Egypt and lead Israel out of slavery (Exodus 3:11; 4:1, 10).

5. Aaron claimed he simply threw the collected gold into the fire and "out came this calf" when confronted about creating an idol (Exodus 32:22–24).

6. The ten spies tried to excuse Israel from going into the Promised Land because there were giants there (Numbers 13:31–33).

7. Israel tried to excuse their rejection of God's rule by saying they wanted a king so they could be like the other nations of the world ("everybody's doing it"?) (1 Samuel 8:5).

8. King Saul tried to excuse his sin of performing priestly duties by saying his army was deserting, Samuel was late, and he—Saul—needed to know what God wanted him to do (1 Samuel 13:11–12).

9. King Saul, after a battle, spared a king whom he was sent to kill and brought back spoils he was told by God to destroy, "in order to sacrifice them to the LORD" (1 Samuel 15:21).

10. Elijah excused his cowardice by hiding in a cave because he was convinced he was the only believer left in Israel (1 Kings 19:10).

11. An unfaithful servant attempted to dodge his blame by saying he knew his master was tough (Matthew 25:24–25).

12. Three different guests excused themselves from attending God's great feast because they wanted to tend to their land, their livestock, and their family (Luke 14:18–20).

13. Felix excused postponing a decision about accepting Christ because he was frightened (Acts 24:25).

I FIND THE DEFENDANT . . .

Israel offered a double system of justice in its courts. Leaders appointed judges to handle civil and criminal cases. Priests dealt with religious matters. All lawsuits came before the judge, and frequently the people seeking justice represented themselves.

The judge listened to the complaint and the defense, then ruled on the matter. People who rejected or tried to evade the ruling could be executed.

In cases such as murder, two or more eyewitnesses had to agree on what they saw to convict a murderer. He or she might then be executed by stoning, either by the victim's family, by professionals appointed by the court, or by a group solicited for that purpose.

Lawyers interpreted the law and might prosecute or defend the various people involved in a charge. There were several layers of lower courts whose decisions might be appealed to higher authorities (see Deuteronomy 1:15–17). However, appeals were granted only when a lower judge could not reach a decision.

JESUS, OLD AND NEW

By some scholars' accounting, there are more than three hundred prophecies in the Old Testament that were fulfilled by Jesus. Some of these prophecies are precise predictions. That is, they specify exactly what would happen and make it clear this is about Jesus, the Messiah. For instance, throughout history God spoke of certain people through whose lineage the Messiah would come. He notes Eve, Shem the son of Noah, Abraham, Isaac, Jacob, and Judah, the fourth son of Jacob. Then God narrowed it down until the Jews received a precise picture of who the Messiah would be. Some have said the probability that Jesus could have fulfilled the many prophecies about him—from his birth to his death and resurrection—would be one in gazillions.

Some prophecies were called "types." These involved events or situations that happened to Israel or others, which were finally fulfilled in Jesus. For instance, when God told Abraham to sacrifice Isaac on the mountain, it appeared a simple enough act. But in fact it was a type of an event to come: God sending his own Son, Jesus, in the place of others to die on the cross.

You can find such types all through Scripture. They range from the simple—Israel coming out of Egypt under Moses the same way Jesus left Egypt as a boy after fleeing there from Herod with his family—to the sublime: Jonah languishing in the belly of the fish for three days and three nights. Jesus himself said he would be in the belly of the earth for the same period of time (see Matthew 12:40).

Several significant prophecies that Jesus fulfilled follow:

1. He would in some special way be born of a woman (Genesis 3:15).

2. He would be from the line of Abraham (Genesis 12:3).

3. He would be from the line of Judah (Genesis 49:10).

4. He would be born of a virgin (Isaiah 7:14).

5. He would reign on the throne of David (2 Samuel 7:11–12).

6. He would be called "Immanuel," "God with us" (Isaiah 7:14).

7. He would be born in Bethlehem (Micah 5:3).

8. He would be worshiped by wise men, and they would give him gifts (Psalm 72:10).

9. He would spend time in Egypt in his early days (Numbers 24:8).

10. Someone would massacre babies from his birthplace (Jeremiah 31:15).

11. He would heal many (Isaiah 53:4).

12. He would speak in parables (Isaiah 6:9–10).

13. He would be rejected (Isaiah 53:3).

14. He would enter Jerusalem in triumph (Zechariah 9:9).

15. His miracles wouldn't be believed (Isaiah 53:1).

16. A friend would betray him for thirty pieces of silver (Zechariah 11:12–13).

17. He would be crucified between two thieves (Isaiah 53:12).

18. His hands and feet would be pierced (Psalm 22:16).

19. Soldiers would gamble for his garments (Psalm 22:18).

20. None of his bones would be broken (Exodus 12:46; Psalm 34:20).

21. His burial place would be a rich man's tomb (Isaiah 53:9).

22. He would rise from the dead (Psalm 16:10).

23. He would ascend into heaven visibly (Psalm 34:7–10).[10]

Is there anyone else in history who has fulfilled all of these prophecies?

THE NEW TESTAMENT ACCORDING TO KIDS

How Sunday school kids answered questions about the Bible:

Q: Who was Mary, and what did she do?

A: When Mary heard that she was the mother of Jesus, she sang the Magna Carta. Jesus was born because Mary had an immaculate contraption.

Q: What was the Golden Rule? Who followed Jesus?

A: Jesus enunciated the Golden Rule, which says to do one to others before they do one to you. The people who followed the Lord were called the twelve decibels.

Q: What are the epistles? Who was Matthew? Paul?

A: The epistles were the wives of the apostles. One of the opossums was St. Matthew, who was also a taxi driver. St. Paul cavorted to Christianity. He preached holy acrimony, which is another name for marriage. A Christian should have only one spouse. This is called monotony.

CLASSIC EDUCATION

The ability to read and write in Old Testament times was common, though no specific government programs sanctioned a public education like we have today.

Jews tried to indoctrinate their children in the Jewish faith. Among the rich, parents employed personal tutors or teachers who worked one-on-one with the children. Most of the instruction from Abraham's time was done in the home (the first home-schoolers?). God commanded parents to teach their children all the stories, laws, and truths of their faith (see Deuteronomy 6:4–9). Moses ordered the Jewish people to write the law on their doorposts. As a result, scholars believe that many people learned writing from their parents.

After the Babylonian exile ended about 516 B.C., because Solomon's Temple had been destroyed and there was no central place of worship, synagogues arose and became the focal point of worship, instruction, and schooling in the community. Normally a teacher would take on twenty to thirty students (probably all male) and would instruct them in the three Rs—reading, writing, and 'rithmetic—using the Old Testament as the primary text.

By the time of Jesus, schools, traveling tutors, and rabbis all served to make general means of instruction available. Based on various things he did as written in the Gospels, Jesus knew how to read and write (see Matthew 5:18; John 8:2–11). Memorization, catechisms, lists, and the like were the primary subjects that were taught.

Probably all of Jesus's disciples could read and write, though some like Peter and John were rough fishermen who might have learned such things as children in their homes. It's possible that Peter couldn't read and write and used an amanuensis (a scribe or secretary) to transcribe his words, because scholars believe Mark wrote the book of Mark according to Peter's dictation, and the books of Peter specifically say Silvanus transcribed Peter's words (see 1 Peter 5:12 NASB).

DEFENSELESS SHEEP

"The LORD is my shepherd, I shall not be in want. He makes me lie down in green pastures, he leads me beside quiet waters, he restores my soul" (Psalm 23:1–3).

That God is our shepherd suggests that we are like sheep. Jesus even refers to us as his sheep in several places (see John 10:26–31). Have you ever seen a sheep? Ever watched them, studied them? Well, then you know being called a sheep is no compliment. But it does reveal an important truth: sheep have absolutely no way to defend themselves against predators; they must depend entirely on their shepherd.

In the same way, we as Christians should not think we can fight against our enemies—the flesh, the world, the devil—on our own. We need Christ's power, presence, and leadership at all times.

CREATION LEGENDS

Most cultures of the ancient world devised creation stories that conflict with what we know from science today. For instance, the Egyptians thought the sun was God. The Mesopotamians believed the universe was created from a dead goddess's body. The Greeks proposed the universe always existed and was run by "fate" with a pantheon of fickle, unruly gods who fought, committed sins, and made a debacle of their worlds. We now know these "theories" are all scientifically untrue. How then did Moses avoid making such huge errors in Genesis 1 that could have made it instantly laughable like these other propositions? For one reason only: because Moses received these truths by revelation from God himself.

AMERICAN LEADERS ON THE BIBLE

Patrick Henry, American patriot: "The Bible is worth all the other books which have ever been printed."

John Adams, second president of the United States: "I have made it a practice every year for several years to read through the Bible."

Ronald Reagan, fortieth president of the United States: "The meaning of the Bible must be known and understood if it is to make a difference in our lives, and I urge all Americans to read and study the Scriptures. The rewards of such efforts will help preserve our heritage of freedom and signal the message of liberty to people in all lands."

Robert E. Lee, Confederate general in the United States Civil War: "The Bible is a book in comparison with which all others in my eyes are of minor importance; and which in all my perplexities and distresses has never failed to give me light and strength."

William Lyon Phelps, American educator: "I thoroughly believe in a university education for both men and women; but I believe a knowledge of the Bible without a college course is more valuable than a college course without the Bible."

MARY MAGDALENE UNVEILED

Despite some of the hubbub today surrounding such books as *The Da Vinci Code,* which make much of Mary Magdalene being the wife of Jesus and the beginning of his lineage up to modern times, not much is known about her from the New Testament. These facts are recorded.

1. Her name probably came from the Galilean town of Magdala.

2. Jesus cast seven demons out of her (Mark 16:9; Luke 8:2).

3. There is no reason to believe Mary was the "sinful woman" referred to in Luke 7:36–39, because Luke certainly would have identified her.

4. Mary appeared at Jesus's crucifixion with several other women who came from Galilee (Matthew 27:55–56).

5. As told in John 20, she arrived at the tomb first (v. 1) and informed Peter that Jesus had risen from the dead (v. 2). She remained for some time alone after the others departed, weeping (v. 11). At that point, she saw two angels (v. 12) and finally Jesus himself (v. 14). It is then that Jesus asked her why she was weeping, and a vibrant exchange occurred (vv. 15–17). Following her meeting with Jesus, she informed the disciples she had seen him (v. 18).

There is no mention of Mary's being married to Jesus, or even of his having a special love for her beyond other women. In fact, John says that Jesus loved Mary, Martha, and Lazarus (see John 11:5) and the disciple John himself (see John 21:7), but no references are made in the Bible about his love for Mary Magdalene. Even according to the literature outside the New Testament that references Mary, it is highly questionable whether any claims can be made that she was married to Jesus.

However, she goes down in biblical history as the first person to see Jesus resurrected and to spread the news about him to others.

DEAR CHILD OF MINE

Next time you read the Bible, set your mind to read it as if it were a letter written to you personally by God. You might try this with Paul's writings, particularly Ephesians or Philippians, or even the letters to Timothy and Titus. Remember as you read that God not only gave the Bible to the world at large, but to you in particular, and that he can open your eyes to his truth in a way that people without faith can never experience.

Reading it that way will show you much about God's personal love and care for you as his follower, friend, and family member.

THE HERODS RULED

Jesus was born about 5 B.C., near the end of the reign of Herod the Great. When Herod died in 4 B.C., his three sons divided his empire. Archelaus took Judea and

Idumea, formerly known as Edom, territory east of Judea by the Dead Sea. Philip gained Iturea, northeast of Palestine on the opposite side of the Jordan River from Israel. Herod Antipas received Galilee and Perea, which was a small parcel of land east of the Jordan, opposite Samaria and Judea.

Herod Antipas, whom Jesus called "that fox" in Luke 13:32, reigned in Galilee from 4 B.C. until A.D. 39. Various intrigues killed off Archelaus in Judea in A.D. 6, and the Romans appointed various governors in his place. Pontius Pilate became governor in A.D. 26, a few years before the time of Jesus's death. During Jesus' trials, he sent Jesus to Herod Antipas, going back and forth among priests and governors several times before Pilate finally sentenced Jesus to crucifixion.

RELIGIOUS NITPICKERS

Some scholars believe the Pharisees began through the Maccabean revolt of 165 B.C. By Jesus's time, three religious/political groups existed in Israel: the strict, legalistic Pharisees, of whom the apostle Paul was one; the politically minded Sadducees, who owned much of the wealth and wielded most of the legal power; and the ascetic Essenes, who lived in the desert and had little influence. By far, the Pharisees were the most respected among the people because of their strict compliance with Moses's law and their deep piety.

The word *Pharisee* means "separatist" or "separated one." They dedicated themselves to follow the Mosaic law so strictly that they turned into eternal nitpickers, attempting to regulate everything in the practices of the believing Jews. Thus the people felt put under tremendous burdens and hardships, morally and spiritually. Because of the excesses of the Pharisees, Jesus said to the people, "Come to Me, all who are weary and heavy-laden, and I will give you rest. Take My yoke upon you and learn from Me, for I am gentle and humble in heart, and you will find rest for your souls, for My yoke is easy and My burden is light" (Matthew 11:28–30 NASB). He implied that he had come to set right religious practice by making it easier and also more joyful and peaceful.

The Pharisees opposed Jesus initially because they believed he broke the Sabbath. He healed people on the day of rest, as well as doing many other things that infuriated them, because they felt the Sabbath was the keystone of their faith. Jesus defended his teachings with common sense—if a lamb fell into a pit on the Sabbath, wouldn't his master rescue it? Nothing he said quelled the Pharisees' vigorous and angry attitudes. Eventually, they decided Jesus committed blasphemy by claiming to be the Son of God. For that, they crucified him.

Today, the Hasidic sects of modern Judaism remain closest to the ideas and practices of the Pharisees of Jesus's time.

GOOD GUYS OF THE BIBLE (1)

There are so many that I've broken this into two lists (in order of appearance).

1. Abel, second son of Adam and Eve, was a man of faith who revered God and followed his ways (Genesis 4). Hebrews 11:4 says God considered him righteous and that though he is now dead, his legacy lives on.

2. Enoch walked with God so closely that God finally whisked him up to heaven at the age of 365 (Genesis 5:21–24).

3. Noah was righteous in God's eyes, and when God decided to end the world and start over, he called Noah to be first father. Noah built the ark, endured the flood, and became an ancestor of everyone in the world today (Genesis 6–9).

4. Abraham, the father of the Jewish people, was the person God chose whose sons would bring God's Word and Messiah to the world (see history starting in Genesis 12).

5. Isaac and Jacob, the first and second generational sons from Abraham, had many flaws but ended up as men of faith who are looked upon with respect as the patriarchs (Genesis 12–50).

6. Joseph, one of the truest men of faith who endured many wrongs at the hands of his brothers and others, emerged as one of the leaders of Israel and a prophetic picture (type) of the Savior of Israel, Jesus Christ (Genesis 39–50).

7. Moses, the great leader of Israel during its time of slavery, is sometimes called the greatest leader in human history. He wrote the first five books of the Old Testament (Genesis, Exodus, Leviticus, Numbers, and Deuteronomy), sometimes called the Law of Moses, or the Pentateuch.

8. Joshua, who took over the leadership of Israel from Moses, conquered the

land of Canaan and established Israel firmly and securely in the "land of milk and honey" (Joshua).

9. The judges of Israel, including Gideon, Samson, Barak, Omri, Othniel, and Deborah, kept Israel together during a dark period in their history without a king (Judges).

10. Samuel, the last judge of Israel, anointed its first kings (Saul and David) and helped establish Israel as a true nation among the nations (1 and 2 Samuel).

THE GREAT FLOOD

One of the most amazing things archaeologists and others have discovered over the years is how many flood stories exist in different cultures. Some have chronicled at least 250 such stories spread all around the world. One could speculate that everyone has a flood story—you should hear Aunt Sarah's!—but the problem is how so many of these stories are similar. We find these stories among the Sumerians, Babylonians, Greeks, Chinese, Algonquin Indians, Hawaiians, Mexicans, and Hindus, to name only a few. Almost every story confirms similar details to the one we find in Genesis 6–9: this man (in some stories he is actually named, though the names are different than Noah) is told to build a boat, for a flood is coming; he builds it, withstands the destruction, and even offers sacrifices to his gods after leaving his boat. His god says he's sorry he had to do it, but sin is sin, and then he offers the man a promise of some sort that he'll never do it again.

The remarkable similarities to the Genesis story are great, and befuddling to humanity. But what other explanation is there than that Noah's family, as they spread throughout the world, would have told such stories around the campfire, dinner table, and barstool?

But what makes the Genesis story the right one? Several things. First, the Genesis account is much more specific, providing dates, names, ages, details about the size of the ship, and so on. Others leave some of these things out. The Babylonian story speaks of a "cubically shaped" ark, which could not have survived such a flood. In some stories, the rain only lashes the earth for seven days, not enough to create the devastation required. The Genesis story also speaks of other sources of the water, including springs and fountains. The Babylonian story says that the flood waters receded in a single day. Quite impossible. At the end, the hero gains immortality from his god for his devotion and obedience. In the Genesis story, Noah gets drunk. Who would have supplied such a detail but the one who wanted to tell the truth?

What all the flood stories do is confirm the authenticity of the Genesis story. Something big happened back then, and the memory of the children of Noah and those who followed was keen. "Have I told you about this great flood my great-great-grandfather went through?" Why would there be such a memory with so many similar details if it was all made up in each culture from scratch?

THE TOWER OF BABEL

Much modern evidence points to humankind having a single original language.

Linguists even depend on this fact as they attempt to build a family tree of the more than six thousand languages employed on earth. Is there any corroboration of the story of the Tower of Babel in other literature?

Incredibly, there is. The Sumerians offer the details on a monument unearthed in Ur. It reveals that Ur-Nammu, the king of Ur from about 2044 to 2007 B.C. decided to build a tower or ziggurat to his god Nannat. Different texts reveal, first, that the attempt to build this gigantic skyscraper offended the gods; second, the gods came down and scattered the people throughout the world; and third, they caused changes in their speech that made them unable to communicate with each other.

This is an amazing confirmation of the biblical story down to the smallest details.

In the end, modern philologists, those who study language and its roots, believe there was only one language throughout the world originally. Such scholars as Alfredo Trombetti, Max Müller, and Otto Jespersen all attest to it, with Jespersen suggesting that God himself gave humankind their first language from which all others have come.

RITES AND RITUALS

Many critics claim that the rites and rituals that inhabited Hebrew worship could not have been instituted as early as Moses. Rather, they say, they came very late in Jewish history, only as the faith matured and the religious ideas became more solidified. They also believe many historical details, like Abraham's battle in Genesis 14 against five cities, had to be made up.

However, the Ebla Tablets, unearthed in Syria by Dr. Paolo Matthiae, an archaeologist, and Dr. Giovanni Pettinato, an epigrapher from the University of Rome from 1964 to 1974 tell another story. More than seventeen thousand tablets have been unearthed. What have they found?

For instance, in Genesis 14 where Moses wrote of Abraham's victory over Chedorlaomer and the Mesopotamian kings, critics claim that the five cities of the plain (Sodom, Gomorrah, Admah, Zeboiim, and Zoar) could only be legends. However, from the tablets researchers found all five cities of the plain mentioned. On one tablet, the list carried the same sequence as the one in Genesis 14. The tablets show that these cities were prosperous and powerful, a culture similar to the one referred to in Genesis.

The tablets also confirmed many of the religious practices of the heathen dating from before 2000 B.C. to be quite consistent with the biblical details, including temple cults, priestly rituals, and different kinds of sacrifices. There are references to such temples as those of Dagon, Astar, Kamos, and Rasap, all mentioned in the Bible.

DOWN TO THE WORDS THEMSELVES

Another astonishing archaeological discovery faces off against various accusations that the Hebrew Bible uses all kinds of words that were unknown until after 600 B.C. Thus, Moses, writing around 1400 B.C., could not have known or used them.

Once again, archaeology whacks this proposition to pieces. Among the words cited by critics as impossibly "late" in origin were

nase—"leader" in the Ebla tablets (2300 B.C.), *nasi* in Hebrew

kutim—"gold" in the tablets, *hetem* in Hebrew

ti'amatum—"deep" in Ebla, *tehom* in Hebrew

irisatum—"desire" in Sumerian/Ebla, *ereshet* in Hebrew, used only once in the Bible

hadath—"be new" or "to renew" in Ugaritic, *hadash/hiddesh* in Hebrew

The German "higher" critics of the nineteenth century made much of these words, saying unequivocally that they proved Moses could not have written the books of the law. But once again, archaeologists have delivered a haymaker to them, much as Paul wrote in Romans 1:18 (NASB): "For the wrath of God is revealed from heaven against all ungodliness and unrighteousness of men who suppress the truth in unrighteousness." These arrogant critics not only "suppressed" the truth, but called it rank lies. In the end, though, they were exposed as the liars. With the Bible, before calling it a fraud, a fake, and full of errors, one should give God a little time to dredge up some squinty-eyed archaeologist who will start digging somewhere and show all such critics what fools they are for attacking God's Word on false pretenses.

THE LONGEST SIX HOURS IN HISTORY

The crucifixion began about 9 a.m. (see Mark 15:25), which is called "the third hour" because morning officially began at 6 a.m., the "first hour," by the Jewish method of keeping time. (The Romans began with midnight, so that "the third hour" would have been 3 a.m.) Jesus expired at the "ninth hour," about 3 p.m. Thus, he hung on the cross about six hours, an unusually short execution, since many crucifixions lasted days. The victim usually died from such things as blood loss, exhaustion, fever, or thirst. Executioners often broke the legs of their victims, as they did with the two thieves who were crucified with Jesus, to cause them to asphyxiate. When a criminal was crucified, the executioners nailed or tied him in a position so that he could push himself up by straightening his legs to breathe, since the position of his arms out and his body hanging left him unable to breathe normally. Thus, victims would push up with their legs, breathe, then relax till the next breath. This made crucifixion especially excruciating, which from the government's point of view was the main point.

When victims were left hanging on a cross for days, they were often eaten alive by birds and beasts of prey, another hideous aspect of the torturous form of punishment. Jesus, however, did not die by the typical means. His legs were not broken, as had been prophesied in Psalm 34:20. In Matthew 27:50 (NASB), Matthew wrote that Jesus "yielded up" his spirit. Many interpret this to mean that Jesus could not have been killed by the crucifixion, but that he gave up his life to the Father as a payment for the sins of the world. That may be the primary reason his execution was abnormally short.

CROSS YOUR FINGERS

Originally, sociologists believe, crossing your fingers—an act of wishing for luck ("I've got my fingers crossed") or to be able to tell a lie without consequence ("Hey, I had my fingers crossed")—was actually a Christian custom in the years after Jesus' death and resurrection. It was use to picture Jesus's cross. Christians used it to identify one another in public.

DEEP DARKNESS

When Jesus died on the cross, the New Testament says darkness covered the land (see Matthew 27:45) from 12 p.m. to 3 p.m. Thallus, a Samaritan historian writing around A.D. 52, mentioned this darkness. He wrote that it was witnessed all over Israel and possibly the whole Roman Empire. He suggested it was an eclipse of the moon. However, historians have found an eclipse was impossible.

No one knows why such darkness came over the land. However, it might have been a judgment of God on the murderers of Jesus, as a kind of warning about who he was—the Son of God, and no ordinary man. God had used darkness before as a judgment, most memorably on the Egyptians through the ninth plague, which was a "darkness that [could] be felt" (Exodus 10:21).

On another occasion, God spoke the commandments to Israel from the mountain shrouded in deep darkness (see Deuteronomy 4:11). Such events were considered a judgment of God for disobedience (see Deuteronomy 28:29; Isaiah 8:22).

When God halted the Egyptian army at the edge of the Red Sea so they couldn't attack the Israelites as they crossed, he threw them into turmoil by cloaking them with a deep darkness (see Joshua 24:7).

Darkness was also portrayed as a time when evil reigns, as Jesus said in Luke 22:53.

God's final judgment on people because of their sin and rejection of his Son will be for them to be "plunged into darkness" where they will "[gnaw] their tongues in agony" (Revelation 16:10).

Clearly, for whatever reasons the darkness appeared on the afternoon of Jesus's crucifixion, it certainly demonstrated God's anger and judgment on those who crucified his Son.

THE DA VINCI ERROR

Leonardo da Vinci (1452–1519), the original Renaissance man, was an architect, scientist, inventor, writer, and painter. He mastered many areas of study, but perhaps his greatest fame comes from two paintings, the "Mona Lisa" and "The Last Supper" of Jesus. In the latter, though, Leonardo made a major mistake. He pictured Jesus sitting at a table with his twelve disciples, all seated on chairs. The problem is that in Jesus's day, diners did not sit at tables, but lay around a much lower table or mat, with their elbows on pillows supporting their heads. In all fairness, many paintings of that era make the same mistake, not to mention the one by Salvador Dali in the twentieth century.

HOW GOD ENABLED MEN TO WRITE HIS WORD (5)

Here we come to the Bible's idea of what inspiration is. From the Scripture passages cited earlier, we see several qualifications, among them these:

- God didn't "dictate" the Bible to the writers; rather, he used their personalities and uniqueness and style as part of the process.

- God didn't "take control" of them so that they slid into a trance or turned into robots or anything like that. No, once again, he used their minds in a supernatural way we can't completely understand and guided them subtly but powerfully to write what he wanted on papyrus or other media without allowing them to foist their own opinions and ideas off on us.

- God didn't allow them to say anything he wouldn't, but on the other hand he occasionally used their "opinions" because their opinions were his opinions!

Do you see how this could have happened? It's ultimately the same thing God does in all of us as he leads us through life. He doesn't force us to do his will but leads and guides and woos and helps us in subtle, almost imperceptible, ways so that his will gets done. He never whips in and bats us over the head, then clobbers us into performing like lions in a cage. Nor does he possess us, turning us into zombies, so that we function like computer programs in which certain code, dictate what we do.

No, he deftly and delicately works with us, us in him and him in us, using our personalities, ideas, desires, and concerns, to bring it to the conclusion he wants. When we fail, he redeems. When we disagree, he woos. When we rebel, he disciplines.

But he never coerces us to do anything.

He inspired the Scriptures in the same way.

Do you see the marvel here? If God had dictated his Word, then the Bible's writers were just secretaries in his hands. If he possessed the writers so they were like computer chips, it's as if they really didn't matter at all. And if he just took what they wrote and worked around it to use it where he could, Scripture loses the divine element, God's stamp of power and life.

But God did none of the above. Instead, he made people an integral part of the process! He let humans share the task with him like partners, even equals!

That's amazing and also humbling. God is not afraid to employ humans to get his work done! That's you and me!

This is one of the hallmarks that separates Christianity from almost all other faiths and beliefs. We have a God who is intimately involved with us, who is personal and who really cares, not just a Master who gives orders, a Boss who lays down rules, or a King who demands our perfect obedience.

TWINKLE, TWINKLE

A minister on an airplane asked the passenger next to him, "What's your occupation?"

"I'm a professor of astronomy. What about you?"

"I'm a pastor," the minister answered.

The astronomer looked uncomfortable but said, "I used to attend church when I was young, but my wife and I don't go very often now. The way I look at it, the Bible is pretty simple. It all boils down to 'Get along with your neighbors and stay out of trouble.'"

"Not bad," said the pastor. "That's similar to how I feel about astronomy. It all boils down to 'Twinkle, twinkle, little star, how I wonder what you are.'"

ANSWERS AND BLESSINGS

Just about any question you need an answer to about moral or ethical living is in Scripture. If you have a nagging difficulty and you need help, the first (and cheapest) place to go to is the Bible. If you obey its directives, God says over and over that you will be blessed by him personally: "How blessed is the man who does not walk in the counsel of the ungodly, nor stand in the path of sinners, nor sit in the seat of scoffers! But his delight is in the law of the LORD, and in His law he meditates day and night" (Psalm 1:1–2 NASB).

TONGUE IN CHEEK (OR FOOT IN MOUTH)

"Now that there's no more praying allowed in school, the kids may have to go to motels just to read a Bible." (Unknown)

Woody Allen: "I'm not afraid of dying; I just don't want to be there when it happens."

George W. Crane, psychiatrist: "I gleaned more practical psychology and psychiatry from the Bible than from all other books."

George Gallup, American pollster: "I could prove God statistically."

Dutch Proverb: "God does not pay weekly, but he pays at the end."

Dante Gabriel Rossetti, English poet: "The worst moment for the atheist is when he is really thankful, and has nobody to thank."

Mahatma Gandhi: "I consider myself a Hindu, Christian, Moslem, Jew, Buddhist, and Confucian."

Napoleon: "If you [General Bertrand] do not perceive that Jesus Christ is God, very well then: then I did wrong to make you a general."

COMPARATIVELY SPEAKING[11]

1. Homer's *Iliad* (written about 800 B.C.): The earliest copy we have is from about 400 B.C. All in all, there are about 643 copies in existence.

2. Herodotus's *The Histories* (written about 450 B.C.): The earliest copy we have is from about A.D. 900. There are eight copies remaining.

3. Plato's writings (written about 400 B.C.): The earliest copy is from A.D. 900. About seven copies exist.

4. Julius Caesar's *Gallic Wars* (written before 44 B.C.): The earliest copy is from A.D. 900. We have ten copies left.

5. Tacitus's *Annals* (written about A.D. 100): The earliest copy is from A.D. 1100. Twenty copies survive.

6. Pliny Secundus's *Natural History* (written no later than A.D. 113): The oldest copy is from A.D. 850, with twenty copies in existence.

How does the New Testament compare to these?

It was completely written by A.D. 100. Our earliest copy is a fragment from A.D. 125, with others as early as A.D. 200–325. We have 5,366 Greek copies (the original language of the New Testament), with another 20,000 copies in other languages including Latin, Ethiopic, Slavic, Armenian, and many others.

NOAH'S ARK

As with many biblical events, the flood generates tremendous speculation, argument, and rage. Some claim the flood had to be universal—covering the whole earth—because of what the Bible says. Others believe it was local—only spanning parts of the Middle East. Both views have positives and negatives, and we won't try to solve the debate here because the Bible can be used to prove both points of view, at least to the satisfaction of their proponents.

What Scripture does show is that the human race degenerated from the idylls of the garden of Eden to a state of such bestiality and evil that God decided he had to start over. He gave humanity one hundred twenty years to repent and follow him in faith. At the same time, he zeroed in on one family who actually did revere him: Noah, his wife, and his three sons and their wives. God commissioned Noah to build the ark, giving him very exact instructions, from the length and width to what animals to bring onto it and in what numbers.

Noah built the ark over the next hundred years. Undoubtedly, the work attracted much attention. As Noah and his sons put it together, people came to stare, heckle, talk, question, and laugh. Noah probably preached to them and offered them hope through repentance and faith. Unfortunately, not one person ultimately believed, and the only persons who entered the ark as the rains began were the original eight.

One of the scientific points in the discussion concerns the dimensions of the ark—length, three hundred cubits (a cubit is about eighteen inches); breadth, fifty cubits; height, thirty cubits. Amazingly enough, this is actually the size and configuration of an average cargo ship. It would have no trouble keeping afloat and safe during a raging storm. Some calculate that it would have displaced about twenty thousand tons with gross cargo tonnage about fourteen thousand tons. This equals about 522 railroad stock cars, each of which could hold about 240 sheep. If Noah brought on 2 of each species of animals, of which about 17,600 are known today, only about 188 stock cars would be required. That leaves well over 300 for food, supplies, and other room for waste and so on. It was a remarkable feat, and even by today's standards it was quite possible. Scholars and others may dispute the details, but for all its rare simplicity, the Bible on this point is commendably accurate.

The Bible calculates that the ark was occupied about 371 days. It ran ashore on the mountains of Ararat. In the last century, books were written about explorers who claim to have seen it imbedded in ice there. However, no expedition has convincingly confirmed it is the ark. Perhaps one day soon we will hear of an expedition that will reveal to the world the final empirical truth.

Until then, while some argue about the extent of the flood, one fact remains: as we've mentioned before, there are more than 250 stories throughout the world's cultures that recall a universal flood. Human history repeats the tale of the flood on every side, and the biblical story continues to be the most precise, though not necessarily scientific in the sense that the story does not provide details beyond the basic human elements.

THE OLD TESTAMENT ACCORDING TO KIDS

"In the first book of the Bible, Guinessis, Adam and Eve were created from an apple tree. Noah's wife was called Joan of Ark. Noah built an ark, which the animals came on to in pears. Lot's wife was a pillar of salt by day, but a ball of fire by night."

"The Jews were a proud people, and throughout history they had trouble with the unsympathetic Genitals. Samson slayed the Philistines with the axe of the apostles."

"David was a Hebrew king who fought with the Finklesteins, a race of people who lived in biblical times. Solomon, one of David's sons, had three hundred wives and seven hundred porcupines."

JUST THE TWO OF THEM

Many people know the story of the original creation according to the Bible, but many of the interesting details escape them. Here are several things to consider about the world's first couple.

First, God created Adam from the "dust of the ground," according to Genesis 2:7. God blew his own breath into man's nostrils, and man became "a living being," different from all other creatures in that he had a soul and the "image of God" stamped on him (Genesis 1:26–27). After Adam named all the animals, presumably looking for a possible "helpmate" for himself from them, he didn't find one that was "suitable." God then put Adam into a "deep sleep," removed a rib from his chest, and fashioned the woman from the rib. When Adam awoke, he recognized her as his perfect mate and counterpart and named her Eve (see Genesis 3:20), which means "life" or "living."

God told Adam and Eve to take care of the garden and have children. He also established one rule: they were not to eat of the "tree of the knowledge of good and evil." God devised this test to make sure the first couple were willing to obey him and thus gain eternal life.

Of course, they failed the test. The serpent, possessed by God's enemy, Satan, came to Eve one day in the garden. We don't know how long after their original creation; it could have been a long time, or just a few days, we don't know. The serpent, through a series of questions and suggestions, tricked Eve into eating the fruit because she saw good reasons to do so. Her husband, who apparently stood there looking on, did not object, and he ate the fruit too.

Instantly, they knew their crime. The first thing they became aware of was that they were naked. In shame, they hid themselves, fashioned "aprons" out of fig leaves, and waited for God, perhaps hoping he just wouldn't appear.

When he did, he quickly found out what they'd done (as if he didn't know), and first Adam, then Eve, blamed others: Adam blamed Eve, Eve blamed the serpent, and the serpent simply stood there unable to blame anyone else. God uttered a curse on all three. This curse rendered life difficult and the world inhospitable, perhaps as a means to lead the errant couple back to God, whom they would need to depend on in new ways simply to survive.

In time, Eve gave birth to two sons, Cain and Abel. When the boys grew up, Cain murdered Abel in a fit of jealousy and anger because God accepted Abel's gifts and rejected Cain's. Cain was cursed after this but left the area where Adam and Eve lived and went to the land of Nod, on the east side of Eden. He married (who, we are not told, nor where she came from, though she could have been a daughter of Eve as well) and started his own line of descendents.

Meanwhile, Eve conceived another son, Seth, as well as other sons and daughters, according to Genesis 5:4. Adam lived 930 years (see Genesis 5:5) and died. Little more is said of either of them.

Adam is mentioned nine times in the New Testament, eight of them referring to him as the first man. One of those puts him at the beginning of Jesus's genealogy in Luke 3:38. One other reference relates to Christ. In 1 Corinthians 15:45 Paul said Adam was the first "living being" and the "last Adam"—Jesus—a "life-giving spirit." First Timothy 2:13–14 says that women should not be spiritual teachers because though Eve was deceived, Adam wasn't.

There are also a number of passages that refer to Adam without mentioning his name: Matthew 19:4–8, where Jesus speaks about the first marriage being inviolate; Romans 5:12, which tells how through one man all people sinned.

Eve is mentioned by name only in 1 Timothy 2:13–14.

While many argue that the Adam and Eve story is little more than a myth or legend concocted to give the Hebrews some sense of history and how evil entered the world, it's clear from the various references beyond Genesis that Luke, Jesus, and Paul believed them to be real people. No one really knows how their history intersects with true human history. Were there cavemen and other people before them who were created, though not in God's image? Can the genealogies in the Bible be used to calculate back to the original parents so that a date of creation can be figured out (4004 B.C., according to research by Bishop Ussher—see article that follows on him)? If they really were the first fully human parents, what race were they, and how did the whole panoply of humanity proceed from them?

These and other questions are probably unanswerable. However, anthropologists and paleontologists believe humanity can be traced back to a single pair. This means, regardless of whether you believe Adam and Eve were real people, the whole human race could have come from them—blacks, whites, Asians, Hispanics, Indians, aborigines, and everyone else.

HE DID THE MATH[12]

James Ussher (1581–1656), Archbishop of Armagh, Primate of All Ireland, and Vice-Chancellor of Trinity College in Dublin, was a celebrated scholar in his time. Of everything he wrote, his mark remains in calculating various chronologies in the Bible. He used both Middle Eastern and Mediterranean histories, as well as the Bible itself, to figure out the precise dates of Creation and various other events in Genesis. His work was so exacting that many believers regarded it with nearly as great respect and reverence as the Bible itself. He established that the first day of Creation happened on Sunday, October 23, 4004 B.C., using rather intricate but easily followed arguments. He also showed that God punished Adam and Eve and drove them from paradise on Monday, November 10, 4004 B.C., and that Noah's ark came to rest on Mount Ararat on May 5, 2348 B.C., a Wednesday.

While scientific discoveries of the last few centuries have discredited such findings, and even though many scholars contend that Ussher's calculations do not discredit the Bible in any way, many people today continue to subscribe to his dates. So don't be surprised if you ever have a discussion with an atheistic evolutionist and he asks you with contempt, "So I suppose you believe the world was created in 4004 B.C.?"

THE LOST ARK

The ark was the central object in Israelite worship. Though much of what the famous movie *Raiders of the Lost Ark* says about it is not true, the producers did rely on some real historical details.

The ark was the place where God dwelled among the people of Israel. In the early days as the nation wandered in the wilderness, a "cloud" representing God's presence and the "shekinah glory" of God hung over the ark in the holiest place in the tabernacle, the Holy of Holies. Specifically, the cloud hovered over the mercy seat, a flat area under the wings of the two cherubim that covered the ark. The ark itself was fashioned of acacia wood and covered with pure gold leaf. On the top, two cherubim stood at the two ends, their wings stretched out over it. At both ends on the sides, two golden rings were fixed so that poles covered in gold could be inserted for carrying the ark to another spot. Only priests on foot could carry the ark. God specifically told Moses never to transport it by cart. Only priests on foot.

Inside the ark were three pieces of memorabilia: the stone tablets on which the Ten Commandments were written; a golden jar holding some manna; and Aaron's rod that budded almond blossoms to prove Aaron's supremacy as high priest (see Numbers 17).

The ark sat in the Holy of Holies during stoppages and later resided in Solomon's Temple. No one ever approached this ark except for the priests who carried it from place to place, and the high priest, and he only on certain sacred occasions. A large and thick veil hung between the Holy of Holies and the Holy Place, an outer room where the regular sacrifices took place. All these elements showed God's presence with the people and the special separation between him and them because of sin.

When Jesus died on the cross, this veil was torn from top to bottom, and the Holy of Holies was exposed (see Matthew 27:51). This demonstrated that God had finally come down to live with the people. No more separation between him and them.

In Scripture, the elements of the temple worship represented heavenly realities. The ark pictured God's abiding presence, as well as his mercy and forgiving love toward sin.

When the temple was destroyed in A.D. 70 by the Romans, the ark disappeared and was never seen again. Many have speculated where it might be hidden, but no one has yet discovered it. The movie *Raiders of the Lost Ark* depicted a Nazi expedition that found and sought to use the ark as a "communication device" with God. But the whole story is fiction. It was never a "communication device," but a place for God to dwell on earth.

EENIE-MEENIE-MINEY-MOE?

Why did God choose Moses? Or Paul? Or anyone who wrote part of the Bible?

Scripture reveals God chose these people, not because they were better than anyone else (or even worse), not because they were poetic or lyrical or even good writers stylistically, and not even because they were more dedicated to him than others. In some cases, he chose these people before they were born (see Jeremiah 1:5; Galatians 1:15). In others, he selected them as the need arose (like Habakkuk). Ultimately, we don't know why God chose any of them.

Take a look at the following chart to see the "other" work of some of the people God used to give us the Bible.

PERSON	OCCUPATION	QUALIFICATIONS
MOSES	shepherd	killed a man and ran for his life
DAVID	shepherd	gifted singer, composer, and musician; also a murderer and adulterer
NEHEMIAH	cupbearer	cared about the Jewish people
ISAIAH	prophet	on fire for God
JEREMIAH	nobody	not interested in the job
HABAKKUK	?	had many raging questions
MATTHEW	tax-man	disciple of Jesus
LUKE	doctor	did much of research on Jesus
PAUL	pharisee	hurt a lot of Christians
PETER	fisherman	would do anything for Jesus
JOHN	fisherman	loved Jesus

DEATH WARRANT[13]

In 1810, excavators at the city of Amitorum (now Aguila) in the kingdom of Naples discovered a marble vase in which was concealed a copper plate, written on one side in Hebrew letters and on the other, also in Hebrew, "A similar plate is sent to each tribe." It was discovered to be the "death warrant" of Jesus Christ. The relic was then placed into an ebony box and held in the sacristy of the Carthusians. The warrant reads as follows:

Sentence rendered by Pontius Pilate, acting governor of lower Galilee, stating that Jesus of Nazareth shall suffer death on the cross. In the seventeenth year of the reign of the Emperor Tiberius and on the twenty-seventh day of March, in the most holy city of Jerusalem, during the pontificate of Annas and Caiaphas, Pontius Pilate, governor of lower Galilee, sitting in the presidential chair of the praetorium, condemns Jesus of Nazareth to die on the cross between thieves, the great and notorious evidence of the people saying:

1. Jesus is a seducer.

2. He is seditious.

3. He is the enemy of the law.

4. He calls himself falsely the Son of God.

5. He calls himself falsely the King of Israel.

6. He entered into the temple followed by a multitude bearing palm branches on their heads.

Orders the first centurion, Quintus Cornelius, to lead him to the place of execution. Forbids any person whomsoever, either rich or poor, to oppose the death of Jesus Christ.

The witnesses who signed the condemnation of Jesus are

1. Daniel Robani, a Pharisee

2. Joannus Robani

3. Raphael Robani

4. Capet, a citizen

Jesus shall go out of the city of Jerusalem by the Gate of Struenus.

There are several flaws in this document.

1. No plate like this is known in archaeology.

2. Such a plate, if authentic, would have been included in the New Testament.

3. No competent scholar has ever reported seeing such a plate, nor has any museum or institution claimed to own such a plate.

4. The twelve tribes and their history broke down more than 750 years earlier (B.C.), after the destruction of Israel by Assyria.

5. That a Roman would feel compelled to justify himself to Jews is inconceivable.

THE DISCIPLES DESERT

Jesus warned his disciples that they would desert him in his final hours. He said in Matthew 26:31 to the eleven remaining disciples, after Judas Iscariot had gone to betray Jesus, "This very night you will all fall away on account of me, for it is written: 'I will strike the shepherd, and the sheep of the flock will be scattered.'" Jesus quoted a prophecy found in the book of Zechariah (13:7), which says, "'Awake, O sword, against my shepherd, against the man who is close to me!' declares the LORD Almighty. 'Strike the shepherd, and the sheep will be scattered, and I will turn my hand against the little ones.'" Peter claimed he would never deny Jesus, but Jesus told him on the contrary, he alone would personally deny he even knew Jesus three times (see Luke 22:31–34). This later happened when Peter watched Jesus at trial in Caiaphas's house. All the other disciples simply hid, except John, who reappeared with Jesus's mother, Mary, as Jesus hung on the cross (see John 19:25–27).

THE DISCIPLES' DEATHS

Jesus frequently told his disciples that they would be persecuted because of their faith and commitment to him. He even told Peter how he would die: according to John 21:18–19, by crucifixion. How did the disciples die? Though the New Testament does not record most of their deaths, from tradition we know these facts:

Andrew was crucified on orders from a Roman governor named Aegeates, at Patrae in Achaia. He was tied, not nailed, to a cross, so his suffering would last longer than usual. He died during the reign of Nero, on November 30, A.D. 60.

Bartholomew died at Albanopolis in Armenia. Some traditions say he was beheaded; others claim he was flayed alive and crucified, head downward, because he convinced Polymius, King of Armenia, to believe in Jesus.

James (brother of John) was the first to be martyred, in A.D. 44, on orders of Herod Agrippa I. Agrippa persecuted the church during Passover that year, where, according to Acts 12:1–2, he had James killed with the sword. According to Eusebius, a church father, who heard it from Clement of Alexandria, the accuser who witnessed against James was touched by the apostle's confession. He believed in Christ, and the two were beheaded together.

James the Less was martyred, but where and how is unknown.

John (brother of James) was banished to Patmos during the reign of Emperor Domitian (A.D. 81–96). According to Tertullian, though, they threw John into a vat of boiling oil in Rome, a miracle saved him, and he was not hurt. After Domitian's death, John returned to Ephesus, where he served as an elder and died about A.D. 100. Of all the disciples, he alone was not martyred violently.

Judas Iscariot committed suicide shortly after Jesus's death because of remorse over betraying Jesus (see Acts 1:18–20).

Matthew was believed by some to have been burned, stoned, or beheaded, but no sure tradition concurs.

Peter fulfilled Jesus's prophecy. A story given by Origen says, "Peter was crucified at Rome with his head downwards, as he himself had desired to suffer." Peter reportedly died this way because he did not believe himself worthy to be crucified the same way as Christ.

Philip died at Hieropolis by martyrdom, according to the apocryphal "Acts of Philip," held to be legendary.

Simon the Zealot was executed at Weriosphora in Iberia, according to Moses of Chorene.

Thaddeus was—according to Jerome, writing in the fourth century—sent on a mission to Abgar, king of Edessa. Nothing more is known about him.

Thomas, claims a strong tradition of preaching in India. Such writers as Ephraem Syrus, Ambrose, Paulinus, Jerome, and Gregory of Tours concur. Some say he preached in Mylapore, not far from Madras, and was executed there.

All the disciples except John paid the price of death for their faith in Christ. In many cases torture was used too. While people the world over have died in defense of their countries or kings (as, for instance, soldiers), few in history have died specifically for beliefs about someone like Christ. Each of the disciples could easily have recanted their statements about Jesus. That none of them did is testimony to the truth of that message and its history.

JOSEPHUS ON JESUS

Flavius Josephus wrote his histories early in the second century. He offers some amazing thoughts about Jesus.

> About this time lived Jesus, a wise man, if it be proper to call him a man, for he was a doer of wonderful works—a teacher of such men as receive the truth with pleasure. He drew over to him both many of the Jews and many of the Greeks. He was the Christ. And when Pilate, at the instigation of the principal men

among us, had condemned him to the cross, those who had loved him at first did not forsake him. For he appeared to them alive again on the third day, the divine prophets having foretold these and many other wonderful things concerning him. And the sect of Christians, so named after him, are not extinct to this day.

Josephus was a Jew. He never converted to faith in Christ.

JESUS'S RESURRECTION BODY

From the biblical account of Jesus's resurrection, we have several details as clues to what he looked like and could do after he rose from the dead:

1. The disciples saw he had a real body—John 20:19–20: "On the evening of that first day of the week, when the disciples were together, with the doors locked for fear of the Jews, Jesus came and stood among them and said, 'Peace be with you!' After he said this, he showed them his hands and side."

2. He could be recognized—John 20:25–29:

   The other disciples told [Thomas], "We have seen the Lord!"
   But he said to them, "Unless I see the nail marks in his hands and put my finger where the nails were, and put my hand into his side, I will not believe it."

A week later his disciples were in the house again, and Thomas was with them. Though the doors were locked, Jesus came and stood among them and said, "Peace be with you!" Then he said to Thomas, "Put your finger here; see my hands. Reach out your hand and put it into my side. Stop doubting and believe."

Thomas said to him, "My Lord and my God!"

Then Jesus told him, "Because you have seen me, you have believed; blessed are those who have not seen and yet have believed."

3. Jesus could do many everyday acts: In Luke 24 he ate some fish (vv. 42–43); he could be touched (v. 39); he spoke to the disciples and spent time with them (vv. 13–31); he broke and ate bread (v. 30); he made a fire and gave the disciples a lunch of broiled fish (see John 21:9–10).

4. Jesus performed some supernatural deeds too: He appeared out of nowhere in certain places and rooms (see John 20:26); he caused the disciples to catch many fish miraculously (see John 21:4–6); he ascended bodily into the air before the disciples and disappeared in the clouds (see Acts 1:9); he did many other things not written down (see John 20:30–31).

One strange detail remains about Jesus's body after the resurrection: people occasionally did not recognize him: Mary Magdalene at the tomb (see John 20:11–18); the disciples on the road to Emmaus (see Luke 24:1–49).

WANTED: PROPHET OF GOD

God usually "called" a prophet to serve him. Often, God revealed himself to the prophet in a vision, dream, or by other means and commissioned him to do a special job. Moses was the first prophet. However, some people spoke prophetic words before him—Lamech, Enoch, Abraham, Isaac, and Jacob. But none of these people were prophets in the typical, biblical sense.

Moses both "forthtold" and "foretold." He explained the word of God to God's people (forthtelling), and he predicted certain events of the future (foretelling). God called Moses at the burning bush (see Exodus 2–3) and sent him to lead the people of Israel out of Egypt. Other prophets followed, but no one ever became one because of personal interest or simple "inner conviction." Each required an external and experiential call by God. If what the prophet predicted did not come true, he could be proven to be a false prophet, and the people were required by God's law to put him to death (see Deuteronomy 18:14–22).

The test of a true prophet came down to this: Did his predictions come true? Were his sermons and writings in conformity with what was already known about the character and person of God? If both issues were proved true, then the people could be sure he was a true prophet of God. But all his words had to come true, at least those that looked at the immediate future. There was no prophesying on a "curve"—if he "hit" 50 or 60 percent of the time, he could be considered for real. No, if he missed once, he was false.

Becoming a prophet was a serious venture. Cowardly folk looking for a new game or shysters hoping for extra pay need not apply.

RESURRECTION OR RESUSCITATION?

People resuscitated from the dead

1. The son of the widow of Zarephath, raised by Elijah (1 Kings 17:22)

2. The Shunammite's son, raised by Elisha (2 Kings 4:34–35)

3. Man who came back to life when his body touched the bones of Elisha (2 Kings 13:20–21)

4. Son of the widow of Nain, raised by Jesus (Luke 7:14–15)

5. Jairus's daughter, raised by Jesus (Luke 8:52–56)

6. Lazarus, brother of Mary and Martha, raised by Jesus (John 11)

7. Dorcas, a disciple, raised by Peter (Acts 9:40)

8. Eutychus, who fell off a window ledge and died, raised by Paul (Acts 20:9–12)

In contrast to these, Jesus was "resurrected" from the dead. The difference is that these people who were resuscitated would still die at a later date because they had mortal bodies. When Jesus rose from the dead, he would never die again. He had a glorified, eternal body.

JESUS'S JOB

How do we know Jesus was a carpenter?

According to Mark 6:3, as Jesus spoke, several listeners said, "Isn't this the carpenter? Isn't this Mary's son and the brother of James, Joseph, Judas and Simon? Aren't his sisters here with us?" From this passage, we believe Jesus was a carpenter. Joseph, his stepfather, was a carpenter also (see Matthew 13:55). What did Jesus do as a carpenter—fine chairs and tables and desks? Perhaps custom homes or boats?

No, according to Trypho, an early Christian, Justin Martyr (A.D. 100–165) said it was mainly ploughs and yokes!

NO ROOM IN THE CARAVANSARY

What kind of place was the inn that turned away the parents of Jesus when they arrived in Bethlehem? Most likely a caravansary, which was ordinarily a compound built around a water supply to give a place to sleep to traveling merchants, soldiers, pilgrims, and others. The inn that turned away Joseph and Mary probably was filled with camel drivers and muleteers who drank, swapped stories, told jokes, and spent the night reveling. They probably were full of lice and fleas, had serious body odor and bad breath, and would kill you as soon as look at you. So perhaps being born among the animals wasn't quite so bad after all!

YESTERDAY'S NEWS

If biblical headlines were written today . . .

On the Red Sea crossing:

WETLANDS TRAMPLED IN LABOR STRIKE

Pursuing Environmentalists Killed

On David versus Goliath:

HATE CRIME KILLS BELOVED CHAMPION

Psychologist Questions Influence of Rock

On Elijah on Mount Carmel:

FIRE SENDS RELIGIOUS-RIGHT EXTREMIST INTO FRENZY

400 Killed

On the birth of Christ:

HOTELS FULL, ANIMALS LEFT HOMELESS

Animal Rights Activists Enraged by Insensitive Couple

On feeding the five thousand:

PREACHER STEALS CHILD'S LUNCH

Disciples Mystified over Behavior

On healing the ten lepers:

LOCAL DOCTOR'S PRACTICE RUINED

"Faith Healer" Causes Bankruptcy

On healing of the Gadarene demoniac:

MADMAN'S FRIEND CAUSES STAMPEDE

Local Farmer's Investment Lost

On raising Lazarus from the dead:

FUNDAMENTALIST PREACHER RAISES A STINK

Will Reading to Be Delayed

HEAVENLY BODIES[14]

What does the Bible say believers' bodies will be like in heaven?

A specific picture of the supernatural, eternal body is provided by Paul in 1 Corinthians 15:40–44:

> There are also heavenly bodies and there are earthly bodies; but the splendor of the heavenly bodies is one kind, and the splendor of the earthly bodies is another. The sun has one kind of splendor, the moon another and the stars another; and star differs from star in splendor.
>
> So will it be with the resurrection of the dead. The body that is sown

is perishable, it is raised imperishable; it is sown in dishonor, it is raised in glory; it is sown in weakness, it is raised in power; it is sown a natural body, it is raised a spiritual body.

If there is a natural body, there is also a spiritual body.

This passage reveals six elements of a resurrected body, which is what Jesus's body was like at the time of his appearances:

1. It is heavenly, suited for the climate and environment of heaven.

2. It is splendorous, marvelously capable of doing all that is necessary in the heavenly realm.

3. It is imperishable; it cannot decay.

4. It is glorious, incredibly powerful, beautiful, and perfect.

5. It is powerful, imbued with special out-of-this-world abilities.

6. It is spiritual; it perfectly conveys the true thoughts and expression of the inner spirit.

Though these details are somewhat sketchy, they are certainly motivating for any of us down here on the planet who are overweight, overwrought, and overwhelmed!

EVERYBODY'S ON THE SAME PAGE

The Bible has amazing internal agreement despite all sixty-six books of the Bible having been written by about forty authors. They wrote from about 1440 B.C. (Moses) to A.D 95 (John, the book of Revelation). The remarkable thing about their writing is that:

1. They reveal facts and events involving God that book outside the Bible records.

2. They reveal facts and events that many secular books also report.

3. They do not disagree internally about any major questions people of the world ask every day:

   Who are we?
   Where are we going?
   What will happen in the end?
   How did we get here?

Take any forty authors today who are writing about a single subject (say, how we got here) and you will get forty different opinions. Not so in the Bible. It's filled with ideas, rules, and facts, and they all agree. To be sure, there are passages and truths we don't understand (sometimes people call them contradictions), but that doesn't mean such problems can't be resolved. Every day new discoveries in archaeology and other sciences confirm that the Bible is true.

The wondrous fact is that we have an accurate, complete, and life-transforming book—the very Word of God.

At the same time, we have a book that is utterly human, involving all the human difficulties, problems, fears, joys, and hurts of the common person. Because of that, the Bible can help people in any situation at any time in any place on earth. In the Bible we see Abraham behaving badly (lying) and Abraham behaving heroically. In the Bible we find Jacob "the cheater" and David, "the man after God's own heart." In the Bible we discover a man named Saul who so hated Jesus and his people that he stomped around trying to kill or incarcerate any Jew who believed in him. We also see this Saul transformed into the apostle Paul, who became the greatest missionary the world has ever seen.

God has given us an amazing book, one that tells the truth about us, him, Jesus, the world, Satan, life, death, eternity, personal problems, and everything else. We can trust it because it's from God. We can enjoy and love it because it came to us through people. And we can use it to face the troubles of life because it demonstrates over and over that God works in and through regular folks like you and me.

POWER BOOK

If you ever wonder about the power of the Word of God, try on these passages as indications of what kind of power it has:

- can keep us from sin (Psalm 119:11)

- can cut us to the quick (Hebrews 4:12)

- can save us from hell and judgment (Acts 4:11–12)

- can help us rebuild relationships (Romans 12:9–21)

- can give us hope in hard times (Romans 15:4)

- can free us from worry and anxiety (Philippians 4:6–7)

WHAT'S THE POINT?

Ever wonder what a primary purpose of the Bible is? Consider this verse:

"Whatever was written in earlier times was written for our instruction, so that through perseverance and the encouragement of the Scriptures we might have hope" (Romans 15:4 NASB).

SKELETONS IN JESUS'S ANCESTRAL CLOSET

Jesus's genealogy in Matthew 1:1–17 lists some impressive personalities from Israel's finest families, including the patriarchs: Abraham, Isaac, and Jacob; Israel's greatest king: David; and the whole line of Israel's kings thereafter. What is amazing is the character of some of these people. Consider this listing:

Abraham—lied twice to protect himself from those who might wish to take his wife and marry her.

Isaac—lied once to protect himself in the same way his father, Abraham, did.

Jacob—cheated his brother and others on his way "up the corporate ladder." His name, Jacob, means "cheat."

Judah and *Tamar*—she pretended to be a prostitute, he bedded her, but she was his daughter-in-law. They produced twins, and clearly the child in Jesus's line was born of incest.

Rahab—she was a harlot from Jericho.

Ruth—she was a Moabite, a family group founded by Moab, the son of Lot's union with his own daughter when she got him drunk. (His other daughter did the same thing and gave birth to Ammon, the patriarch of another group that fought with Israel.)

David—committed adultery with Bathsheba and then had Bathsheba's husband murdered to cover up his sin.

Solomon—he was an idolater and the world's most prolific polygamist.

Uzziah—he became a leper after disobeying God through pride.

Manasseh—he was a mass murderer and genocidal maniac.

Jeconiah—he was so wicked, God cursed his line.

Clearly, Jesus had a few skeletons in his closet.

IT TAKES A PRO

A woman was at work when she received a phone call that her daughter was very sick with a fever. She left her work and stopped by the pharmacy to get some medication for her little girl.

Upon returning to her car, she found she had locked her keys inside.

She called home and told the babysitter what had happened and that she didn't know what to do.

The babysitter told her that her daughter was getting worse. She said, "You might find a coat hanger and use that to open the door." The woman looked around and found an old rusty coat hanger that had been thrown down on the ground (possibly by someone else who at some time or other had locked his keys in his car).

Then she looked at the hanger and said to herself, "I don't know how to use this." So she bowed her head and asked God to send her some help. Within five minutes an old rusty car pulled up, with a dirty, greasy, muscle-bound man who was wearing an old biker skull rag.

The woman thought, *Great, God. This is what you sent to help me?* But she was desperate, so she was also very thankful.

The man got out of his car and asked her if he could help.

She said "Yes, my daughter is very sick. I stopped to get her some medication and locked my keys in my car. I must get home to her. Please, can you use this hanger to unlock my car?"

"Sure." He walked over to the car, and in less than one minute the car was opened.

She hugged the man and, through her tears, said, "Thank you *so* much. You are a very nice man."

The man replied, "Lady, I am not a nice man. I just got out of prison today. I was in prison for car theft and have only been out for about an hour."

The woman hugged the man again and, still sobbing, cried out loud, "Thank you, God, for sending me a professional!"

CATCHING UP

What is the rapture?

The "rapture" or "catching up" of the saints to meet Christ in the air is referred to in several passages, even though the word itself isn't used in Scripture. *Rapture* comes from the Latin, meaning to be "carried away," which can refer to physical or emotional transport.

Theologically, the rapture is called the "blessed hope" (from Titus 2:13) that will keep Christians from a time of tribulation at the end of time. God will rescue them out of the world at a trumpet call from Christ. The doctrine comes from two passages from Paul's epistles:

Listen, I tell you a mystery: We will not all sleep, but we will all be changed— in a flash, in the twinkling of an eye, at the last trumpet. For the trumpet will sound, the dead will be raised imperishable, and we will be changed. For the perishable must clothe itself with the imperishable, and the mortal with immortality. (1 Corinthians 15:51–53)

Brothers, we do not want you to be ignorant about those who fall asleep, or to grieve like the rest of men, who have no hope. We believe that Jesus died and rose again and so we believe that God will bring with Jesus those who have fallen asleep in him. According to the Lord's own word, we tell you that we who are still alive, who are left till the coming of the Lord, will certainly not precede those who have fallen asleep. For the Lord himself will come down from heaven, with a loud command, with the voice of the archangel and with the trumpet call of God, and the dead in Christ will rise first. After that, we who are still alive and are left will be caught up together with them in the clouds to meet the Lord in the air. And so we will be with the Lord forever. Therefore encourage each other with these words. (1 Thessalonians 4:13–18)

Much debate revolves around the timing of the rapture, whether it's before the "great tribulation," in the middle of it, or after, and whether it happens before the thousand-year reign of Christ. Many interpreters agree on a number of facts about the rapture:

1. An angel will sound a "trumpet" that all the world will hear, including unbelievers, that will begin the rapture.

2. Christ will come unexpectedly, without warning or sign, like a "thief in the night." As a result, Christians must be ready by practicing godly, wholesome habits in their lives, or they will be "caught unaware."

3. All the saints from all time will "meet Christ in the air." This includes Old Testament believers, such as Abraham, David, and Moses, as well as people who trusted in Christ after his appearance.

4. At that moment, saints will be "changed," given a supernatural, spiritual body that is immortal, imperishable, and without taint, utterly perfect.

Scripture has not given us the details of when, where, why, and how the rapture will occur. The main idea is that the rapture is the Christians' "blessed hope"—that we will not all die, but some, at the end of time, will be "translated" into that perfect body without going through death. It is meant as a great encouragement to believers everywhere.

AFRAID OF A NUMBER?

"Antichrist! 666! The end of time! Millions slain! Death to all followers of Christ!"

The number 666 inspires fear in many people. But is "666" something we should fear, worry about, obsess over?

While the number 666 has become a well-known symbol of evil, as well as prophecies about the end of the world, most people probably don't know where it came from or what it means. It does come right out of the Bible. The reference is Revelation 13:18: "This calls for wisdom. If anyone has insight, let him calculate the number of the beast, for it is man's number. His number is 666."

In the book of Revelation, 666 refers to the Antichrist (see entry on Antichrist). Many scholars, researchers, and sensationalists have told us what they think this means. Some add up the numeric values of letters in a person's name. Others suggest that credit cards issued in the time of the Antichrist will contain that number. Over the years, these people have used such methods to prove that names of famous people from Nero, Adolf Hitler, John F. Kennedy, the pope, Ronald Reagan, Bill Clinton, and George W. Bush all fit. When one falls out of the public eye, another replaces him. Today, I'm sure someone has found that Osama bin Laden or Kim Jong-il can be added up that way. I suspect we're all wrong.

No one really knows what the apostle John, the writer of Revelation, was referring to when he said 666 was "man's number." No one knows how this number will appear in human events. The general layout of Revelation, though, does offer a hint. If Revelation is a prophecy of future events near the end of the world as we know it, then as each prophecy unfolds, the meaning of the prophecy will become obvious to the world at that time. People will read Revelation like they might read the daily newspaper. Its words will match world events occurring at that time. Today's reader may see Revelation as shrouded in symbolism and mystery. But when the actual end times arrive, the meanings will become obvious—if Revelation is about the future. Some, though not many, scholars believe Revelation is about past events or purely symbolic.

ONE EXTRAORDINARY STATEMENT

Perhaps Jesus's most extraordinary statement in the Bible, especially for Jewish followers, was the command to "love your enemies" (Matthew 5:43–45). The Jews had some stern ideas about their enemies, even though Moses said in Leviticus 19:18, "Do not seek revenge or bear a grudge against one of your people, but love your neighbor as yourself. I am the LORD."

The Pharisees and leaders of the Jews interpreted this passage to mean something quite different. They said, "You shall love your neighbor and hate your enemy." This expression is never found in Scripture and was not derived from anything God said. In fact, in Proverbs 25:21, God said that people should do good to their enemies. The Jews, though, deleted such ideas and made up their own. This was a big part of their fight with Jesus. In his own way, Jesus reinterpreted their words to bring them into line with truth. Thus, "love your enemies" was born. Undoubtedly, no one much liked it at first, but Jesus backed it up with much sense: love them the same way your father "makes the sun to rise on them" and "sends them rain" regardless of their state of sin and evil.

FIGHTING BACK

Jesus told His followers to turn the other cheek (see Matthew 5:39) and "love your enemies" (Matthew 5:44). From this, many people get the idea that Christians should never fight back when people attack them. However, Jesus wasn't telling us we can't defend ourselves when we're physically attacked. Turning the other cheek applies to insults, not mortal threats. In fact, Jesus himself fought back (verbally, not physically) when people came against him several times, including at his trial before the hostile Jews (see John 18:23). Nothing in the New Testament says we should not stand against evil people or defend ourselves.

JUST MY STYLE

Why did God include so many different forms of writing in the Bible—poetry, history, laws and commandments, stories, parables, teaching, prophecy?

It's more than a matter of keeping us interested and appealing to the human need for variety in life. God knows how short our attention spans are. But on a higher level, he had to give us much information in as fascinating a fashion as possible that could be understood and applied by everyone in every culture in every time. He surely couldn't wait to communicate his word by radio or television because they didn't exist until the twentieth century. Also, he had to consider people at different ages and interests, from young children to elderly men and women, from farmers to entrepreneurs, from soldiers to sinners to saints. In effect, he has put in the Bible something for everyone and for everyone something!

What then do you find in the Bible? Look at the following chart to get a grasp of the spectrum:

BOOK	KIND OF LITERATURE
Genesis	history of the beginning of the world and the Jews
Exodus	God's rules for living
Deuteronomy	Moses's last few sermons to Israel before he died
Ruth	a love story
Job	a true story to help resolve the issue of "Why do good people suffer?"
Psalms	poems and hymns
Proverbs	maxims for wise living
Ecclesiastes	a skeptic wrestles with the great questions
Song of Songs	a love story written as a play for the stage
Isaiah	thundering prophecies about the future and rebukes to Israel about bad behavior
Haggai	motivation to keep building the temple
Luke	the story of Jesus's life, death, and resurrection
John	everything everybody else left out about Jesus' life
Acts	the history of the early church
Romans	a letter to explain God's plan of salvation
Philippians	a letter of encouragement
Revelation	what will happen at the end of time

As you can see, the Bible contains many different kinds of writing. Obviously, God loves variety—just look at all the animals, fish, and birds in the world. He also enjoys telling a good story—simply study the parables of Jesus or the history passages in the Bible. He never sugarcoats or glosses over the details by telling only the good things (as the Egyptians did in their records), but he never gets so down on us that we feel like we're being slammed into the middle of next eternity!

No, he patiently tells the story and then lets us decide if he's worth believing, trusting, and knowing personally.

DIGGING DEEPER

If you'd like to study the Bible more in-depth, consider these Study Bibles as sources of information and personal inspiration:

- *The MacArthur Study Bible* (NKJV) by John MacArthur (editor)
- *The Ryrie Study Bible* (NIV, NASB, and KJV) by Charles Ryrie (editor)
- *The Quest Study Bible* (NIV) by Phyllis Ten Elshof (editor)
- *The Inspirational Study Bible* by Max Lucado (editor)

THAT'S GOTTA HURT!

The book of Job relates how Job suffered in Satan's attack.

1. boils all over his body (2:7)

2. intense itching (2:7–8)

3. grief over losses of wealth and children (2:13)

4. lack of appetite (3:24, 6:6)

5. insomnia (7:4)

6. worms in flesh (7:5)

7. oozing and breaking boils (7:5)

8. hallucinations (7:14)

9. gangrene (13:28)

10. extremely bad breath (19:17)

11. teeth falling out (19:20)

12. skin turning black (30:30)

13. intense fevers (30:30)

14. tremendous weight loss (33:21)

THE LIVING WORD

"The word of God is full of living power. It is sharper than the sharpest knife, cutting deep into our innermost thoughts and desires. It exposes us for what we really are" (Hebrews 4:12 NLT).

In case you're thinking the Bible is boring, outdated, or just not your cup of tea, read the above verse again. The Bible is actually alive in a spiritual sense, and filled with power. No one can long read and study it without it's affecting his or her life dramatically.

JESUS IN LITERATURE

A number of ancient, secular authors mentioned Christ in their writings, often lending proof to the facts of his work and ministry.

- *Tacitus, a Roman historian, born around A.D. 52.* He was governor of Asia, son-in-law of Julius Agricola (governor of Britain in A.D. 80–84). He wrote much of the history of the reign of Nero and mentioned Jesus as well as the fact that there were many of his followers in Rome. He wrote this around A.D. 112:

    But not all the relief that could come from man, not all the bounties that the prince could bestow, nor all the atonements which could be presented to the gods, availed to relieve Nero from the infamy of being believed to have ordered the conflagration, the fire of Rome. Hence to suppress the rumor, he falsely charged with the guilt, and punished with the most exquisite tortures, the persons commonly called Christians, who were hated for their enormities. Christus, the founder of the name, was put to death by Pontius Pilate, procurator of Judea in the reign of Tiberius; but the pernicious superstition, repressed for a time, broke out again, not only through Judea, where the mischief originated, but through the city of Rome also. (Annals, XV. 44)

- *Lucian of Samosata, a satirist of the second century.* Lucian ridiculed Christ and his followers, but mentioned Christ when he wrote: ". . . the man who was crucified in Palestine because he introduced this new cult into the world. . . . Furthermore, their first lawgiver persuaded them that they were all brothers one of another after they have transgressed once for all by denying the Greek gods and by worshipping that crucified sophist himself and living under his laws" (*The Passing of Peregrinus*).

- *Suetonius, a court official and historian under Hadrian.* Suetonius wrote the history of the Imperial House around A.D. 120: "As the Jews were making constant disturbances at the instigation of Chrestus, he expelled them from Rome" (Life of Claudius 25.4).

- *Pliny the Younger, governor of Bithynia in Asia Minor in A.D. 112.* Pliny wrote to Emperor Trajan once, seeking advice on how to deal with the increasing number of Christians in his area. He persecuted and killed them and "made them curse Christ," but stated that "a genuine Christian cannot be induced to do [so]." In the same letter, he said, "They affirmed, however, that the whole of their guilt, or their error, was, that they were in the habit of meeting on a certain fixed day before it was light, when they sang in alternate verse a hymn to Christ as to a god, and bound themselves to a solemn oath, not to any wicked deeds, but never to commit any fraud, theft, adultery, never to falsify their word, not to deny a trust when they should be called upon to deliver it up" (Epistles X.96).

- *Thallus, a Samaritan-born historian.* Thallus wrote in A.D. 52 about Christ. His writings have vanished, but Julius Africanus, a Christian writer, quoted him around A.D. 221, speaking of the darkness that covered Judea during Christ's crucifixion: "Thallus, in the third book of his histories, explains away this darkness as an eclipse of the sun—unreasonably, as it seems to me (unreasonably, of course, because a solar eclipse could not take place at the time of the full moon, and it was at the season of the Paschal full moon that Christ died)."

• A letter from Mara Bar-Serapion is preserved in the British Museum. It was written after A.D. 73 and mentions that certain wise men were often persecuted.

What advantage did the Athenians gain from putting Socrates to death? Famine and plague came upon them as a judgment for their crime. What advantage did the men of Samos gain from burning Pythagoras? In a moment their land was covered with sand. What advantage did the Jews gain from executing their wise King? It was just after that that their kingdom was abolished. God justly avenged these three wise men: the Athenians died of hunger; the Samians were overwhelmed by the sea; the Jews, ruined and driven from their land, live in complete dispersion. But Socrates did not die for good; he lived on in the teaching of Plato. Pythagoras did not die for good; he lived on in the statue of Hera. Nor did the wise King die for good; He lived on in the teaching which He had given.

Of course, many writings of those known as the "church fathers"—Tertullian, Origen, Justin Martyr, the Shepherd of Hermas, the Letter of Barnabas, and others—speak of Christ. Josephus also wrote about Jesus (see Josephus on Jesus).

A BESTSELLING PRAYER

Several years ago, a book called *The Prayer of Jabez* made a big splash in publishing. To date, more than ten million copies have sold. But who was this Jabez, and why is his prayer so monumental?

We find Jabez in 1 Chronicles 4:9–10:

> Jabez was more honorable than his brothers. His mother had named him
> Jabez, saying, "I gave birth to him in pain." Jabez cried out to the God of
> Israel, "Oh, that you would bless me and enlarge my territory! Let your hand
> be with me, and keep me from harm so that I will be free from pain." And
> God granted his request.

Nowhere else do we find his name in the Bible. His name falls in a list of the descendents of Judah, the son of Jacob through whom Jesus ultimately came. But Jabez wasn't actually in Jesus's line.

The main point about him was that he prayed a unique prayer, and God granted his request. Why God answered it positively, we don't know, but Jabez appears to be a man of faith. He also seems to have known how to pray at a time when few men of Israel had any idea what kinds of prayers God honored. So we can certainly assume he was a spiritual man, deeply committed to God, and a man who believed God can answer sincere prayers and do the miraculous.

While his life remains a mystery, as the book *The Prayer of Jabez* suggests, his prayer offers a good template for personal prayer. There are four requests:

- "Bless me," which could be interpreted, "God, bless me with the blessing you choose for me, whatever it might be."

- "Enlarge my territory," or, "Make the arena of life in which I live become larger so that I may influence more people."

- "Let your hand be with me," or, "Enlist me in the work of your kingdom, and use me to advance it."

- "Keep me from harm so that I will be free from pain," meaning, "If you do all these things, I may be attacked by your enemies, so please protect me as I work to make your name known and spread the truth about you to those who don't believe."

Of course, you may have some different interpretations. But don't think this is some self-oriented, "Please give me everything I want out of life" kind of prayer. It's not. As Bruce Wilkinson wrote in *The Prayer of Jabez*, this is a prayer about serving God and making his name known throughout the world. So pray it only if you want to be someone God will use to get the word out about his love and nearness to us.

ANGELS ALL AROUND

On several occasions, angels helped and strengthened Jesus and his family during difficult times.

1. In Luke 1:26, Gabriel appeared to Mary, telling her she would get pregnant with and bear Jesus, the Messiah: "In the sixth month, God sent the angel Gabriel to Nazareth, a town in Galilee."

2. In Matthew 1:20–21, an angel came to Joseph in a dream to assure him of Mary's virgin pregnancy with Jesus: "After he had considered this, an angel of the Lord appeared to him in a dream and said, 'Joseph son of David, do not be afraid to take Mary home as your wife, because what is conceived in her is from the Holy Spirit. She will give birth to a son, and you are to give him the name Jesus, because he will save his people from their sins.'"

3. In Matthew 2:13, an angel warned Joseph in a dream to flee from Israel: "When they had gone, an angel of the Lord appeared to Joseph in a dream. 'Get up,' he said, 'take the child and his mother and escape to Egypt. Stay there until I tell you, for Herod is going to search for the child to kill him.'"

4. In Matthew 2:19–20, an angel advised Joseph in yet another dream that King Herod was dead and he could return to Israel: "After Herod died, an angel of the Lord appeared in a dream to Joseph in Egypt and said, 'Get up,

take the child and his mother and go to the land of Israel, for those who were trying to take the child's life are dead.'"

5. In Matthew 4:11, angels ministered to Jesus after he was tempted by Satan in the wilderness: "Then the devil left him, and angels came and attended him."

6. In Luke 22:43, an angel strengthened Jesus while he prayed in the garden of Gethsemane about his impending crucifixion: "An angel from heaven appeared to him and strengthened him."

7. In Matthew 28:2, an angel rolled away the rock at Jesus's tomb: "There was a violent earthquake, for an angel of the Lord came down from heaven and, going to the tomb, rolled back the stone and sat on it."

8. In Matthew 28:5, either one or two angels appeared to inform the women that Jesus had risen from the dead: "The angel said to the women, 'Do not be afraid, for I know that you are looking for Jesus, who was crucified.'"

YOU WERE THERE

As you read your next passage of Scripture, try to imagine what the writer must have thought and felt as he penned his words. Do you think he was conscious of writing the Word of God? Why, or why not? Do you think the words saddened or encouraged him? How might you feel if you were that person writing God's Word? What kind of reception would you hope for when you passed it on to God's people?

MONSTER PRAYER

An atheist was spending a quiet day fishing, when suddenly his boat was attacked by the Loch Ness Monster. In one easy flip, the beast tossed him and his boat at least a hundred feet into the air. The monster then opened its mouth and waited below to swallow man and boat.

As the man sailed head over heels and started to fall toward the open jaws of the ferocious beast he cried out, "Oh, my God! Help me!"

Suddenly, the scene froze in place. As the atheist hung in midair, a booming voice came out of the clouds and said, "I thought you didn't believe in me!"

"God, come on, give me a break!" the man pleaded. "Just seconds ago I didn't believe in the Loch Ness Monster either!"

"Well," said God, "now that you are a believer, you must understand that I won't work miracles to snatch you from certain death in the jaws of the monster, but I can change hearts. What would you have me do?"

The atheist thought for a minute and then said, "God, please have the Loch Ness Monster believe in you also."

God replied, "So be it."

The scene started in motion again, and the atheist fell toward the ravenous jaws of the ferocious beast.

Then the Loch Ness Monster folded his claws together and said, "Lord, bless this food you have so graciously provided."

EXPRESS YOURSELF BIBLICALLY

"Christianity is antiart!"

"The teachings of the Bible and our beliefs about real art cannot coexist!"

"No, real art emerged through Christian believers! The first art was Christian!"

So what's the truth? Would Jesus have supported the National Endowment for the Arts? Some people believe the Bible does not condone art or artistic expression. They say there is no such thing as art for art's sake. Artistic expression is only to be used in worship.

What of art that pictures people urinating on a cross? Or a woman, covered in chocolate, haranguing people about being antifeminists? For that matter, what about art that isn't at all religious, that simply glorifies the beauty of nature or the world of a blind woman, like the famous painting by Andrew Wyeth, "Christina's World"?

While the Bible condemns blasphemy (ridiculing or mocking sacred things), an antiart bias does not agree with what the Bible really says. Throughout its pages, we find references to craftsmen—men and women skilled in various arts. Whether they worked in metal such as bronze or gold, or whether they skillfully wove high-quality curtains and clothing, the world admired their handiwork.

For instance, Exodus 26:1 refers to the craftsmen who would create the curtains for the Jewish temple: "Make the tabernacle with ten curtains of finely twisted linen and blue, purple and scarlet yarn, with [images of] cherubim worked into them by a skilled craftsman."

Exodus 38:23 also speaks of craftsmen creating artistic fabrics: "With him was Oholiab son of Ahisamach, of the tribe of Dan—a craftsman and designer, and an embroiderer in blue, purple and scarlet yarn and fine linen." Clearly, leaders such as Moses applauded these arts—craftmaking, designing, and embroidery—and used them throughout the Israelite culture.

The Bible does not specifically mention painting and sculpting beyond forbidding the creation of idols. However, archaeological and historical records show us that people created beautiful objects out of pottery, metal, and stone at every level of life. Admiring and enjoying beautiful things is right out of Paul's words in the book of Philippians (4:8): "Finally, brothers, whatever is true, whatever is noble, whatever is right, whatever is pure, whatever is lovely, whatever is admirable—if anything is excellent or praiseworthy—think about such things."

Also, the book of 1 Corinthians talks extensively about "spiritual gifts" (see 1 Corinthians 12–14). Though most of the gifts involve church fellowship and helping people become better Christians, could not God also gift people with artistic abilities meant to benefit all of us—through paintings, banners, dramatic presentations, music, and so on?

Ask yourself this: Do you love beautiful things? Do you enjoy art? Undoubtedly, God gifted you in certain ways, whether it's sculpting or gardening, drawing or making music. The Bible encourages you to develop your gifts. Learn more. Take classes. Then take your gift as far as you can go. Do the best you can. The Bible tells us that God is in favor of art, as much as he is in favor of faith and salvation.

MIRACLES FOR A GRUMPY PROPHET

Here's a list of the miracles found in the book of Jonah:

1. God sent a great wind on the sea to stop Jonah from fleeing (1:4).

2. When the lots were thrown, the right one pointed out Jonah as the culprit (1:7).

3. God stopped the hurricane (1:15).

4. God prepared a great fish to rescue Jonah (1:17).

5. The fish swallowed Jonah (1:17).

6. God made the fish vomit Jonah up onto dry land (Jonah 2:10).

7. Nineveh repented en masse (3:10).

8. God made a plant grow up in one day (4:6).

9. God killed the plant with a worm (4:7).

10. God sent a torrid wind upon Jonah (4:8).

While Jonah did not work any of these miracles like Moses, Elijah, Elisha, Jesus, and the apostles did, he experienced the hand of God in ways no one had before or has since.

A BOW AND A BIRD

According to tradition, the apostle John had a hobby raising pigeons. On one occasion a fellow church leader who was returning from a hunting trip stopped by John's place, found him playing with one of his pigeons, and gently corrected him for wasting his time.

John, noticing his friend's hunting bow, said that the string was loose, whereupon the man replied, "Yes, I always loosen the string of my bow when it's not in use. If it stayed tight, it would lose its resilience and fail me in the hunt."

"And I am now relaxing the bow of my mind," said John, "so that I may be better able to shoot the arrows of divine truth."

ANTICHRIST[15]

The term *Antichrist* usually refers to a figure pictured in the book of Revelation as the final political leader seeking to end Christ's influence and power in the world. He will display himself as being God incarnate, and the whole world will follow him—except for those who believe in Christ (see 2 Thessalonians 2:1–4). He will persecute and kill Christians. One of his acts will be to use the number 666 as some special symbol of his person and position. It will be done in a way that will be obvious to people of his time, but which scholars today do not understand. On the basis of the verse referring to it, 666 will be a calculation, perhaps assigning numerical values to the letters of the Antichrist's name or something like that.

However, such people as Adolf Hitler, Joseph Stalin, Richard Nixon, John Kennedy, and Ronald Reagan have all been mentioned (in their times) as antichrists. The real one will give a mark to all who follow him. This mark will appear either on the forehead or on the hand, and without it a person will not be able to buy or sell anything the world over.

He is the ultimate incarnation of evil, sets himself up as being God, and leads all astray who do not believe the truth (see Revelation 12–14). Following him is a sure ticket to hell, according to John's statement in Revelation 14:11: "The smoke of their torment rises for ever and ever. There is no rest day or night for those who worship the beast and his image, or for anyone who receives the mark of his name."

JOHN'S BONES

Churches all over Europe display relics of John the Baptist, including three shoulder blades, four legs, five arms, and fifty index fingers. Clearly, John was either rather grotesque in appearance, or somebody made a lot of money selling "relics" to Christian churches!

A KISS OF DEATH

According to Mark 14:44, Judas Iscariot, one of Jesus's disciples, worked out a deal with the Jews to show them which one in the crowd was Jesus when Judas led them to come and arrest him. Judas said, "The one I kiss is the man; arrest him and lead him away under guard."

Judas had been in the Upper Room earlier with the disciples as Jesus served the Last Supper. At one point, Jesus told him to leave and do what he had to do. Judas left and later led the soldiers to Jesus in the garden of Gethsemane, where Jesus had been praying. An even more illuminating text is found in Luke 22:47–48: "While he was still speaking a crowd came up, and the man who was called Judas, one of the Twelve, was leading them. He approached Jesus to kiss him, but Jesus asked him, 'Judas, are you betraying the Son of Man with a kiss?'"

Apparently, the leaders who came to arrest Jesus didn't know him by sight, or at least they were uncertain in the dark and needed someone to direct them to the right person. Why did Judas choose a kiss? It seems strange to us today, but this was actually a very intimate, loving way to greet a person in those days. Perhaps Judas's own guilt about what he meant to do made him choose this sign because of a deep hatred of Jesus, since it was certainly a despicable way to betray someone.

It may also have been a fulfillment of a prophecy from Psalm 41:9, where David wrote, "Even my close friend, whom I trusted, he who shared my bread, has lifted up his heel against me."

In the story of Jesus's last day, he broke bread with Judas as an honored guest at the Passover dinner that we now call the Last Supper. It was also Judas whom Jesus greeted as a close friend in Matthew 26:50: "Friend, do what you came for."

Perhaps this was Jesus's last attempt to try to bring Judas to his senses, by showing his great love for him, calling him the intimate term "friend," as if to say, "I still think of you as my friend, Judas."

Clearly, Judas didn't accept that title. He died by suicide later that weekend.

HAPPY BIRTHDAY!

Is December 25 Jesus's birth date? It might be, since it has to be one of 366 possible dates. But there's actually no proof. The date came about through Dionysius Exiguus, who made up the Easter Tables and put Jesus's birth date as December 25.

That day was also the day celebrated as a pagan holiday to the sun, which the Romans created as a day of feasting for the people. After Constantine's conversion to Christianity in A.D. 312, he wanted to turn all pagan celebrations into Christian special events. This was his way of Christianizing paganism. Until Dionysius's dating, January 6 was used as the day of Christ's birth. Today, Eastern Orthodox Christians still celebrate that date as Christmas.

Nonetheless, neither date can be proved to be the birth date of Christ, since Scripture indicates nothing about it, not even that his birth occurred in winter, in December or January, and certainly not on a Roman feast day for the sun. However, there is some irony in this since Jesus called himself "the light of the world" (John 8:12) and could realistically be posed as the new "sun" of God!

FEMINISM AND THE BIBLE

Many Christians fight against modern feminism. They say it has destroyed the sanctity of the family and supports such things as immorality and the war of the sexes.

The truth is, modern feminism actually has its roots in the Bible. In biblical times, women were regarded as little more than slaves. A Pharisee thanked God every day, saying, "Thank you, Lord, that you did not make me a tax collector, a Gentile, or a woman."

This attitude didn't exist just among the Jews. In other nations, women had no real choices. Their husbands or fathers had total control over them. Young girls were often given to older men solely for the purpose of providing children. The husband met his sexual needs elsewhere. In some places, people claimed women didn't even have souls and had no right to heaven or a joyous eternity.

However, throughout Jewish history, prophets raged against the poor treatment of women. Malachi cried out that God hated divorce, something that men could get on nearly any whim (see Malachi 2:16).

King Solomon wrote the Song of Songs as an anthem to the love relationship. In Proverbs, he told his son,

> *Drink water from your own cistern,*
> *running water from your own well.*
>
> *Should your springs overflow in the streets,*
> *your streams of water in the public squares?*

Let them be yours alone,
never to be shared with strangers.

May your fountain be blessed,
and may you rejoice in the wife of your youth.

A loving doe, a graceful deer—
may her breasts satisfy you always,
may you ever be captivated by her love. (Proverbs 5:15–19)

The Bible regards women as sacred symbols of love in family life. Still, many didn't get the message.

Jesus clarified it even further. Some of his closest friends were women. Mary and Martha, the sisters of Lazarus, to name two, became beloved intimates. Jesus always showed compassion to women as his conversation with the woman at the well shows (see John 4). Jesus's response to the prostitute who brought an alabaster jar of perfume to give to Jesus in the presence of some condemning Jewish leaders demonstrates his love and respect for all women (see Luke 7:36–50). When the Jews used a woman caught in an affair to try to trap Jesus, Jesus had mercy on the woman and preserved her life (see John 8:1–11). Jesus regarded women as joint heirs of God's blessings. He broke the prejudice the Jews had against women. Some of the greatest members of the early church mentioned in the New Testament were women, including several who became leaders.

Paul himself, often vilified as a woman hater, said that women were equals with men in the eyes of God: "There is neither Jew nor Greek, slave nor free, male nor female, for you are all one in Christ Jesus" (Galatians 3:28). He told husbands to love their wives "as Christ loved the church" and to sacrifice themselves for their wives, treating them with the same respect and love they give their own bodies (see Ephesians 5:25–33).

Peter called a wife a joint heir of the "grace of life" (1 Peter 3:7 NASB). A man's prayers could actually be hindered if he mistreated his wife.

What of women having careers and making their own mark on the world?

The Bible applauds women who use their minds and abilities to accomplish good things for their families and others. Proverbs 31 is a picture of praise for the woman who resourcefully enters into business and makes a profit for her household. Lydia, one of the first converts in the church at Philippi was a "dealer in purple cloth," a businesswoman in her own right and well respected (see Acts 16:13–15). The Bible mentions other women with notes of respect and love (see Romans 16; Philippians 4:2–3). Priscilla and Acquila, a committed couple in the early church, taught one of the great orators of the faith, Apollos, in the finer points of theology as a team (see Acts 18:24–26).

While many abuses have occurred over the years, the Bible supports many of the claims of modern feminists. Their right to a career, success, and all the trappings of power are accorded to them should they want it. A good, loving marriage was a Christian right. And even the right to sexual fulfillment is established in the book of Corinthians: "The husband should fulfill his marital duty to his wife, and likewise the wife to her husband" (1 Corinthians 7:3).

God is not against women on any level. He created women as equals to their men and honors them as joint heirs of eternity and all the riches God will give his people at the end of time. Yes, feminists have taken some things to extremes. But the best virtues of the movement—the equality of women and their rights and privileges—are right out of the mouth and teachings of Jesus.

GOOD GUYS OF THE BIBLE (2)

11. *Jonathan,* the friend of David and son of King Saul, David's great enemy, helped David out of many scrapes and proved to be the quintessential friend of human history and legend (1 Samuel).

12. *David,* the "sweet psalmist" and first great king of Israel and a true warrior, consolidated the kingdom under his authority, conquered many peoples, and led Israel into a golden age (1 and 2 Samuel).

13. *Solomon,* son of David, became the richest, wisest man on earth in his time, resulting from his deep faith and wise answer to God when God asked, "What do you want?" (1 Kings).

14. *Jehoshaphat,* king of Judah from 873–848 B.C., was a man of faith who prevented at least one great disaster for Judah in battle by consulting with God's prophet rather than the idolatrous prophets of King Ahab of Israel (1 Kings 22:1–50).

15. *Elijah,* prophet to Israel, performed many miracles, prophesied to the evil king Ahab continually, and was finally taken up into heaven on a flaming chariot (1 Kings 17:1–2 Kings 2:11).

16. *Elisha,* protégé to Elijah, went on in his power and ministry and performed more miracles and prophesied to the evil kings of Israel (2 Kings 1:1–8:15).

17. *Hezekiah,* great king of Israel from 715 to 686 B.C., returned Israel to God and expressed great faith in God when Sennacherib, king of Assyria, attacked Jerusalem. Sennacherib was defeated by a miraculous plague (2 Kings 18:1–20:21).

18. *Josiah,* king from 640 to 609 B.C., rediscovered the law of Moses and reinstituted the Jewish religion; a man of great faith and commitment (2 Kings 22:1–23:30).

19. *Daniel,* Shadrach, Meshach, and Abednego were all young men taken into exile by the Babylonians. They served in King Nebuchadnezzar's palace and were party to many miracles and prophecies of the end times of the world (Daniel).

20. *Hosea,* prophet of Judah from 755 to 710 B.C., became a great example of God's love for his people through his disastrous marriage to Gomer, who repeatedly committed adultery, while he remained faithful (Hosea).

OF SAINTS AND SINNERS

Two brothers had terrorized a small town for decades. They were unfaithful to their wives, abusive to their children, and dishonest in business. The younger brother died unexpectedly.

The surviving brother went to the pastor of the local church. "I'd like you to conduct my brother's funeral," he said, "but it's important to me that during the service, you tell everyone my brother was a saint."

"But he was far from that," the minister countered.

The wealthy brother pulled out his checkbook. "Reverend, I'm prepared to give $100,000 to your church. All I'm asking is that you publicly state that my brother was a saint."

On the day of the funeral, the pastor began his eulogy this way: "Everyone here knows that the deceased was a wicked man, a womanizer, and a drunk. He terrorized his employees and cheated on his taxes." Then he paused.

"But as evil and sinful as this man was, compared to his older brother, he was a saint!"

WAS JESUS REALLY BORN OF A VIRGIN?[16]

There are several references in Scripture to Jesus's being born of a virgin. The prophecy cited is from Isaiah 7:14, in which Isaiah tells King Ahaz, one of the errant kings of Israel, "The Lord himself will give you a sign: The virgin will be with child and will give birth to a son, and will call him Immanuel."

The word here used for "virgin" is the Hebrew word *almah* and can mean "virgin, young woman, or maiden," though it normally refers to a woman who is not yet married. However, the prophecy seems to apply to two events: a young woman giving birth to a son during King Ahaz's time (fulfilled by Isaiah's son; see Isaiah 8:3); and a virgin giving birth to the Messiah, who would be called "Immanuel," which means "God is with us." These kinds of double fulfillments were common in the Old Testament.

When Matthew cited the reference in Matthew 1:23, he quoted the passage from the Septuagint, a Greek translation of the Old Testament made by loyal Jews living in Egypt in the 300s B.C. In Matthew's quotation, there is no ambiguity in the meaning of the term for "virgin," the Greek word, *parthenos*, which always means a virgin, a young woman who has never had sexual relations.

The only other references to Jesus's virgin birth occur in Luke 1:26–38 where the Virgin Mary is told by the angel Gabriel she will conceive a Son who is to the Savior and King of the Jews. When she questions the angel, she learns she will conceive through the power of the Spirit and remain a virgin. The purpose of this was so that her Son would be both completely human and divine, and also without sin.

These are the only passages clearly delineating the doctrine of the virgin birth of Christ. One other passage, though, indicates the Jews might have known some of the circumstances of Jesus's birth. We find in John 8:41, where Jesus accuses the Pharisees of being born of the devil, this exchange taking place:

"You are doing the things your own father does," [Jesus said.]

"We are not illegitimate children," they protested. "The only Father we have is God himself."

In another passage, Mark 6:3, Jesus is referred to as "Mary's son," as if there was a cloud of suspicion hanging over the nature of Jesus's birth.

The reference to illegitimate children could be an oblique accusation that they thought Jesus was illegitimate. This is congruent with Jewish tradition that Jesus was born illegitimately.

The virgin birth is a key doctrine of the Christian faith. Without it, there is no substantial proof that Jesus was anything other than a normal human being, corrupted by original sin and subject to all the infirmities of humankind. How was divinity conferred on him if not through a virgin birth? Also, if he did have original sin and was a sinner like the rest of humanity, how then could he pay for the sins of the world? Would he not have had to pay for his own sins first?

Both sides of the issue have difficult problems to solve. To those believing in a virgin birth is the whole mechanism of how God impregnated Mary and how Jesus could be God and man in one person. To those not believing in it, the problem is how Jesus could be sinless, God and the Savior of the world all in one, without it.

CELEBRATE![17]

In Leviticus 23, six feasts to the Lord were laid out. The sacred year was set up this way:

MONTH	SPECIAL DAY
Nisan (April)	14—Passover 15—Unleavened bread 21—Close of Passover
Iyar (May)	
Sivan (June)	6—Feast of Pentecost or Weeks
Tammuz (July)	
Ab (August)	
Elul (September)	
Tishri (October)	1–2—The Feast of Trumpets or Rosh Hashanah 10—Day of Atonement or Yom Kippur 15–21—Feast of Tabernacles
Marchesvan (November)	
Kislev (December)	
Tebeth (January)	
Shebet (February)	
Adar (March)	

HOW MANY? (NEW TESTAMENT)[18]

According to the statistics gathered by Thomas Hartwell Horne (see "How Many? [Old Testament]"), the King James Version breaks down as follows:

Books: 27

Chapters: 260

Verses: 7,959

Words: 181,253

Letters: 838,380

ON VACATION

Did you know Jesus took spiritual vacations?

There are some who refuse to take vacations or periods of rest, saying, "The devil never takes a vacation." But when you study the Gospels, you'll find at least nine times when Jesus, either alone or with His disciples, went aside to rest, pray, and think.

MATTHEW 14:13: *"When Jesus heard what had happened, he withdrew by boat privately to a solitary place. Hearing of this, the crowds followed him on foot from the towns."*

MATTHEW 14:23: *"After he had dismissed them, he went up on a mountainside by himself to pray. When evening came, he was there alone."*

MATTHEW 26:36: *"Jesus went with his disciples to a place called Gethsemane, and he said to them, "Sit here while I go over there and pray.""*

MARK 1:35: *"Very early in the morning, while it was still dark, Jesus got up, left the house and went off to a solitary place, where he prayed."*

MARK 1:45: *"[The healed leper] went out and began to talk freely, spreading the news. As a result, Jesus could no longer enter a town openly but stayed outside in lonely places. Yet the people still came to him from everywhere."*

MARK 6:31: *"Because so many people were coming and going that they did not even have a chance to eat, he said to them, 'Come with me by yourselves to a quiet place and get some rest.'"*

LUKE 5:16: *"Jesus often withdrew to lonely places and prayed."*

LUKE 9:10: *"When the apostles returned, they reported to Jesus what they had done. Then he took them with him and they withdrew by themselves to a town called Bethsaida."*

JOHN 6:15: *"Jesus, knowing that they intended to come and make him king by force, withdrew again to a mountain by himself."*

(IM)MANUAL LABOR[19]

At the time of Jesus's life on earth, manual work was considered by the Romans and others to be beneath them, something only slaves did. There were more than seven million slaves in the Roman Empire, most of them conquered peoples who were forced to serve demanding masters. They performed all menial, as well as important, duties in the Empire, from washing people's feet when they came to visit, to acting as physicians, teachers, and tutors. Jesus's work as a carpenter became for all the ages a symbol of the importance and goodness of such work.

In fact, Jesus had quite a bit to say about work, including several parables:

The Weeds (Matthew 13:24–30) is a parable in which Jesus shows that Satan tries to foil the work of God's kingdom, but the workmen should be patient, knowing God will sort the true from the bad at the end.

The Unmerciful Servant (Matthew 18:23–35) warns masters and overseers to be kind and gentle, or Christ will punish them for their evil ways.

The Hiring of the Workers in the Vineyard (Matthew 20:1–16) demonstrates that God is always looking for people to work in his kingdom and that he will give them all eternal life and reward regardless of how much of their lives they actually did work.

The Two Sons (Matthew 21:28–32) pictures two sons, one of whom said he'd perform his father's work but didn't, and the other who refused, then went and did it anyway. Jesus shows here that deeds are more important than impetuous words.

The Wicked Tenants (Matthew 21:33–45) exposes all who would scandalize God's kingdom by hurting his servants. It warns any who attack God's workers that God will deal with them personally.

The Talents (Matthew 25:14–30) is a parable in which Jesus told people to be faithful to the gifts God has given them, to invest and use them wisely for the kingdom of God, as God will one day reward them for their work.

The Rich Fool (Luke 12:16–21) is about a successful businessman who has great income and wealth but fails to give God a place in his life. He ends up losing his soul for his oversight.

The Tower Builder (Luke 14:28–30) shows the importance of planning and making sure you can see a project through before you ever start it.

The Lost Sheep (Luke 15:3–7) pictures a shepherd who cares so much for the one that has gotten away that he goes out and retrieves him.

The Shrewd Manager (Luke 16:1–8) illumines the importance of using your power, position, and possessions for advancing the kingdom.

The Rich Man and Lazarus (Luke 16:19–31) demonstrates the shallowness and folly of worldly might and wealth when not shared and used for the kingdom of God.

Very clearly, Jesus was concerned about how people used their time and money in their work. In the letters of Paul, you also find many admonitions about the glory and privilege of work:

EPHESIANS 6:5–8: *"Slaves, obey your earthly masters with respect and fear, and with sincerity of heart, just as you would obey Christ. Obey them not only to win their favor when their eye is on you, but like slaves of Christ, doing the will of God from your heart. Serve wholeheartedly, as if you were serving the Lord, not men, because you know that the Lord will reward everyone for whatever good he does, whether he is slave or free."*

COLOSSIANS 3:22–24: *"Slaves, obey your earthly masters in everything; and do it, not only when their eye is on you and to win their favor, but with sincerity of heart and reverence for the Lord. Whatever you do, work at it with all your heart, as working for the Lord, not for men, since you know that you will receive an inheritance from the Lord as a reward. It is the Lord Christ you are serving."*

I TIMOTHY 6:1–2: *"All who are under the yoke of slavery should consider their masters worthy of full respect, so that God's name and our teaching may not be slandered. Those who have believing masters are not to show less respect for them because they are brothers. Instead, they are to serve them even better, because those who benefit from their service are believers, and dear to them. These are the things you are to teach and urge on them."*

There are also admonitions to employers as well.

IDLE THREAT

Satan's threat to God (Isaiah 14:12–14):

1. He would "ascend to heaven"—face off with God in God's personal residence.

2. He would "raise [his] throne above the stars of God"—he would take God's place as leader of the angels.

3. He would "sit enthroned on the mount of assembly"—he would take God's throne and conduct business in heaven as if he were God.

4. He would "ascend above the tops of the clouds"—he would go into God's most sacred and personal place, presumably to kill God.

5. He would "make [himself] like the Most High"—he would completely eliminate God from power and take over the spiritual universe.

In other words, Satan boasted that he would do nothing less than murder God.

THE TWELVE TRIBES OF ISRAEL

Jacob, the son of Isaac and Rebekah, fathered twelve sons and one daughter, Dinah. Jacob had two wives, Leah and Rachel. These two wives fought continually, because Jacob loved Rachel but not Leah. The girls' father, Laban, tricked Jacob into marrying Leah first, because she was the older. Leah produced the first four sons: Reuben, Simeon, Levi, and Judah. Then she suddenly stopped conceiving.

Meanwhile, Rachel, her sister and rival wife, had no children. But Rachel thought of a way to give Jacob children: she gave her handmaiden, Bilhah, to mate with Jacob so she could adopt whatever children resulted. Bilhah soon gave birth to Dan and Naphtali.

Not to be outdone, Leah tried the same tactic and gave Jacob her handmaiden, Zilpah. Two more sons resulted, Gad and Asher. At that point, Leah made a deal with Rachel so that she could sleep with Jacob again, and Rachel gave in. Leah conceived and produced two more sons, Issachar and Zebulun.

Finally, after all that time, God opened Rachel's womb. She gave birth to two sons, Joseph and Benjamin.

One more time Leah conceived and gave Jacob a daughter, Dinah.

Thus, the lineage looks like this, with birth order in parentheses:

THROUGH LEAH, UNLOVED WIFE OF JACOB

> Reuben (1)
>
> Simeon (2)
>
> Levi (3)
>
> Judah (4) (line of Jesus)
>
> Issachar (9)
>
> Zebulun (10)

THROUGH BILHAH, HANDMAID OF RACHEL

> Dan (5)
>
> Naphtali (6)

THROUGH ZILPAH, HANDMAID OF LEAH

> Gad (7)
>
> Asher (8)

THROUGH RACHEL, LOVED WIFE OF JACOB

> Joseph (11)
>
> Benjamin (12)

All Jews were born through one of these twelve tribes. In the days of Jesus, there were books in the temple that traced the lineage of every living Jew back to Abraham. Books of the Old Testament like Numbers and 1 and 2 Chronicles contain long genealogies from these twelve tribes. The New Testament features two genealogies of Jesus, one in Matthew 1, and a second in Luke 2.

COULD JESUS EVER COMMIT A SIN?

Could Jesus have committed a sin if he had wanted to? Could he have been tempted and given in, as movies such as *The Last Temptation of Christ* have tried to show?

A doctrine called the "impeccability of Christ" is the answer to this question. "Impeccability" comes from the French terms, *in* and *peccare*, which means to be incapable of sin, to be entirely without fault. This means Christ not only was able not to sin, but was also not able to sin in any form. The idea of the doctrine comes from the following Scripture verses:

HABAKKUK 1:13: *"Your eyes are too pure to look on evil; you cannot tolerate wrong."*

2 CORINTHIANS 5:21: *"God made him who had no sin to be sin for us, so that in him we might become the righteousness of God."*

HEBREWS 4:15: *"We do not have a high priest who is unable to sympathize with our weaknesses, but we have one who has been tempted in every way, just as we are—yet was without sin."*

JAMES 1:13: *"When tempted, no one should say, 'God is tempting me.' For God cannot be tempted by evil, nor does he tempt anyone."*

I JOHN 1:5: *"This is the message we have heard from him and declare to you: God is light; in him there is no darkness at all."*

I JOHN 3:5: *"You know that he appeared so that he might take away our sins. And in him is no sin."*

From these scriptures we see that not only was Jesus sinless in that he never committed sin, but he was also incapable of committing sin. The problem some have with this is that if Christ could not sin, he also could not truly be tempted. If so, then how can he be an example to us of one who has faced temptation and triumphed? If he could not sin, the issue was closed. He cannot really understand what we face during temptation, nor can we learn from him as an example of one who can defeat temptation.

From passages like Matthew 4:1–10, where Satan "tempted" Jesus in the wilderness, we find no evidence that Jesus was not truly tempted. Certainly, Satan believed he could make Jesus fall or he would not have tried. In other passages (see Hebrews 2:17–18 and 4:15–16) we learn that Jesus was tempted "in every way, just as we are—yet was without sin." How then can these two ideas—being incapable of sinning and yet being truly tempted to sin—be reconciled?

It is the idea of "testing" and "tempting" that must be understood. The Greek word *peirasmos* can mean either "testing" or "tempting." When something is tested, two results are possible: success or failure. Someone may be tested over and over with success every time, but the test remains real in each situation. A successful "test" proves a person or thing can stand the pressure. Achieving success every time does not mean the pressure wasn't there or that the test was somehow bogus.

Thus, while Jesus was tested completely and always met success, every test was real and put pressure on him that he had to withstand. Because he always met with success, he knows how to help people at any stage in the process—those undergoing an easy test, a moderate test, a difficult test, or an excruciating test. He knows how to succeed in all situations and thus can help people in all situations.

But, some may ask, didn't Jesus ever experience guilt, failure, frustration, or the agony of defeat?

Yes, on the cross he experienced all the emotions, feelings, and psychological ramifications and agonies of complete failure before God. When Jesus hung on the cross, the sin of the world was placed on him in some mystical way by God the Father, and Jesus experienced the full impact of sinful humanity. He became spiritually separated from the Father, went to the place of eternal damnation, and knew all the agonies of what it is to commit sin in the eyes of a holy God. Such scriptures as these confirm his experiences:

MATTHEW 27:46: *separation from God through the experience of personal guilt and sin through the sins of the world being laid on him*—"*About the ninth hour Jesus cried out in a loud voice, 'Eloi, Eloi, lama sabachthani?'*—which means, 'My God, my God, why have you forsaken me?'"

ISAIAH 53:12: *all the results of sin, suffering, disease and pain through humankind's sin being laid on him*—"*I will give him a portion among the great,*

270

and he will divide the spoils with the strong, because he poured out his life unto death, and was numbered with the transgressors. For he bore the sin of many, and made intercession for the transgressors."

MATTHEW 8:17: *"This was to fulfill what was spoken through the prophet Isaiah: 'He took up our infirmities and carried our diseases.'"*

I PETER 3:18–20: *the agonies of hell—"For Christ died for sins once for all, the righteous for the unrighteous, to bring you to God. He was put to death in the body but made alive by the Spirit, through whom also he went and preached to the spirits in prison who disobeyed long ago when God waited patiently in the days of Noah while the ark was being built."*

While in many ways what happened on the cross to Christ remains a mystery that only study in eternity will enable us to fully fathom, the truth remains that Jesus experienced all the depths, deceptions, tricks, and tribulations of true testing and tempting. When we go to him, we can be sure we will find a sympathetic, informed, helpful, and empowering Savior.

GO TELL IT ON THE MOUNTAIN

The following is a list of mountains of Israel:

1. Mount Ararat, where Noah's ark stopped (Genesis 8:4)

2. Mount Seir, where Esau lived after the death of Isaac (Genesis 36:8)

3. Mount Sinai (or Horeb), where Moses received the law (Exodus 19:2–25)

4. Mount Ebal, where an altar was built as Israel entered the land of Canaan (Deuteronomy 27:4)

5. Mount Pisgah, the last place from which Moses saw the Promised Land (Deuteronomy 34:1)

6. Mount Hermon, which stood farthest north in Israel (Joshua 11:3, 17)

7. Mount Zion, where Jerusalem was built (2 Samuel 5:7)

8. Mount Lebanon, where cedar for Solomon's Temple was cut (1 Kings 5:14)

9. Mount Carmel, where Elijah proved God was the true God of Israel (1 Kings 18:9–42)

10. Mount Gilboa, where King Saul committed suicide (1 Chronicles 10:1, 8)

11. Mount Moriah, where Abraham was to sacrifice Isaac (Genesis 22:2); also the place where Solomon's Temple was built (2 Chronicles 3:1)

12. Mount of Olives, where Jesus gave his sermon on his second coming (Matthew 24:3)

13. Mount Gerizim, where Jesus spoke with the woman at the well (John 4:20)

COMING AGAIN

Jesus spelled out the details of his second coming in one major passage, Matthew 24:27–31:

> As lightning that comes from the east is visible even in the west, so will be the coming of the Son of Man. Wherever there is a carcass, there the vultures will gather.
>
> Immediately after the distress of those days
>
> *"the sun will be darkened,*
>   *and the moon will not give its light;*
> *the stars will fall from the sky,*
>   *and the heavenly bodies will be shaken."*
>
> At that time the sign of the Son of Man will appear in the sky, and all the nations of the earth will mourn. They will see the Son of Man coming on the clouds of the sky, with power and great glory. And he will send his angels with a loud trumpet call, and they will gather his elect from the four winds, from one end of the heavens to the other.

You can find more details about his second coming in other passages:

ACTS 1:10–11: *"They were looking intently up into the sky as he was going, when suddenly two men dressed in white stood beside them. 'Men of Galilee,' they said, 'why do you stand here looking into the sky? This same Jesus, who has been taken from you into heaven, will come back in the same way you have seen him go into heaven.'"*

REVELATION 1:7: *"Look, he is coming with the clouds, and every eye will see him, even those who pierced him; and all the peoples of the earth will mourn because of him. So shall it be! Amen."*

REVELATION 19:11–16: *"I saw heaven standing open and there before me was a white horse, whose rider is called Faithful and True. With justice he judges and makes war. His eyes are like blazing fire, and on his head are many crowns. He has a name written on him that no one knows but he himself. He is dressed in a robe dipped in blood, and his name is the Word of God. The armies of heaven were following him, riding on white horses and dressed in fine linen, white and clean. Out of his mouth comes a sharp sword with which to strike down the nations. 'He will rule them with an iron scepter.' He treads the winepress of the fury of the wrath of God Almighty. On his robe and on his thigh he has this name written: KING OF KINGS AND LORD OF LORDS."*

From the above scriptures, at least these details can be known about the second coming of Christ:

1. He will come on a horse with the armies of heaven.

2. Every eye will see him, even those who brutalized him on the cross.

3. As he comes, he will gather all his saints together to be with him.

4. He will set up his kingdom and reign forever.

Many people today are asking, Will this happen soon? Jesus himself provided the answer in Matthew 24:32–39:

> Now learn this lesson from the fig tree: As soon as its twigs get tender and its leaves come out, you know that summer is near. Even so, when you see all these things, you know that it is near, right at the door. I tell you the truth, this generation will certainly not pass away until all these things have happened. Heaven and earth will pass away, but my words will never pass away.
>
> No one knows about that day or hour, not even the angels in heaven, nor the Son, but only the Father. As it was in the days of Noah, so it will be at the coming of the Son of Man. For in the days before the flood, people were eating and drinking, marrying and giving in marriage, up to the day Noah entered the ark; and they knew nothing about what would happen until the flood came and took them all away. That is how it will be at the coming of the Son of Man.

Perhaps the best way to prepare is from Jesus's words in Matthew 24:44: "So you also must be ready, because the Son of Man will come at an hour when you do not expect him."

• • •

A priest was called away for an emergency. Not wanting to leave the confessional unattended, he called his rabbi friend from across the street and asked him to cover for him. The rabbi told him he wouldn't know what to say, but the priest told him to come on over and he'd stay with him for a little bit and show him what to do. The rabbi showed up, and he and the priest sat in the confessional.

In a few minutes, a woman came in and said, "Father, forgive me for I have sinned."

The priest asked, "What did you do?"

The woman said, "I stole money and lied."

"How many times?"

Woman, "Three times."

Priest, "Say two Hail Mary's, put five dollars in the box, and go and sin no more."

A few minutes later, a man enters the confessional. He says, "Father, forgive me for I have sinned."

Priest, "What did you do?"

Man, "I stole money and lied."

Priest, "How many times?"

Man, "Three times."

Priest, "Say two Hail Mary's, put five dollars in the box, and go and sin no more."

The rabbi tells the priest that he thinks he's got it, so the priest leaves.

A few minutes later, another woman enters and says, "Father, forgive me for I have sinned."

Rabbi, "What did you do?"

Woman, "I stole money and lied."

Rabbi, "How many times?"

Woman, "Once."

Rabbi, "Go do it two more times. We have a special this week, three for five dollars."

THE SEA OF WEIRD WEATHER

Located in the northeast section of Israel, the Sea of Galilee, also known as Gennesaret and Chinneroth, is thirteen miles long and seven miles wide. At 675 feet below sea level, its fresh waters are home to many fish, making it (in Jesus's day) the largest source of food in the north of Israel. The River Jordan connected it to the Dead Sea in the south.

Because it's surrounded by mountains, storms frequently strike unexpectedly. The mountains funnel the wind down into the sea and often catch seasoned fishermen out on it. In fact, on several occasions, Jesus performed miracles that involved this strange weather pattern of sudden raging storms and high seas. In one, he "walked on water" and in another he stilled a storm that had arisen quite suddenly (see Matthew 14:22–33; Mark 4:33–41).

JESUS'S LIFE

About 5 B.C.—Birth in Bethlehem (Matthew 2:1–11; Luke 2:1–7)

About A.D. 6—first Passover in Jerusalem (Luke 2:41–50)

About A.D. 27—baptism by John and beginning of ministry (Matthew 3:13–17)

A.D. 27

    Winter—John the Baptist ends; Jesus begins

    Spring—first Passover as a teacher, healer, and miracle worker

    Summer—Nicodemus and Jesus talk (John 3)

A.D. 28

    Winter—disciples called

    Summer—Jesus goes throughout Galilee

    Fall—Sermon on the Mount (Matthew 5–7)

A.D. 29

    Winter—more ministry in Galilee

    Spring—third Passover

A.D. 30

    Winter—Jesus goes throughout Perea

    Spring—last Passover; last week of life

death on the cross and resurrection (Matthew 26–28)

Forty days on earth after resurrection

Ascension (Acts 1)

JESUS'S MIRACLES

The New Testament records many of the miracles of Jesus and his disciples. You can find thirty-five separate miracles Jesus performed in the Gospels. There are several different kinds. One involves the healing of illness. Jesus healed blind, deaf, mute, and crippled people of all kinds. Most of the miracles were instantaneous and unchangeable. The lame walked. The blind saw. The deaf heard. The leprous were made clean. As far as we know, these people didn't walk away and a few days later find the miracle "didn't take." No, as far as we know, they were all permanent.

A second kind of miracle called for the casting out of demons. Many times, Jesus sent out anywhere from one demon to a multitude of them from individuals who were immediately set free.

A third kind of miracle might be called the "helping" miracle, where Jesus did something to help others. He changed water into wine at Cana, fed the five thousand, fed the four thousand, and sent Peter to retrieve some tax money from a fish's mouth.

A fourth kind of miracle involved raising people from the dead. Jesus raised three dead people: the widow of Nain's son (see Luke 7:11–15), the daughter of Jairus (see Matthew 9:18–26), and Lazarus (see John 11:17–44).

The New Testament tells us these were not the limits of Jesus's miracles (John 21:25). Rather, these were the ones mentioned in the Bible. We know Jesus performed multitudes of other miracles of which we know few details, except for passages like Matthew 4:23: "Jesus went throughout Galilee, teaching in their synagogues, preaching the good news of the kingdom, and healing every disease and sickness among the people." Jesus may have done hundreds of other miracles that are lost to history.

While some say these miracles were "healings" of psychosomatic illnesses or fakes, the problem for such critics is threefold: the amazing variety of the miracles; the fact that there were many eyewitnesses who could have disputed them later; and the time of the report. The Pharisees and Sadducees never refuted Jesus's miracles or even tried to. Rather, they said he did them by the power of Satan.

Moreover, all his miracles were reported matter-of-factly like newspaper reporting, without embellishments. That is, Jesus never engaged in theatrics or tricks when he performed a miracle. He simply spoke and it happened—instantly. The witnesses were often skeptics until they finally saw these things happen.

DEMONS AND DEVILS

What is the difference between demons and devils?

Devil means "slanderer" in Greek. *Demon* can be translated "evil spirit." Generally, the writers used them interchangeably. However, *devil* pictures activity—slandering God, Jesus, God's people. *Demon* represents a spiritual state.

THE FLOOD: BEGINNING TO END

The book of Genesis lays out the story.

1. God told Noah to build the ark (Genesis 6:14).

2. Noah went into the ark in his six hundredth year (second month, tenth day (7:4, 10–11).

3. The flood began seven days later (7:11).

4. The rain went on for forty days, but the floodwaters remained on the earth for 150 days (7:12, 17, 24, 8:1).

5. The waters receded until the Ark rested on Mount Ararat (8:4).

6. By Noah's six hundredth year, tenth month, first day, the mountains were visible (8:3–4).

7. Another forty days later (six hundredth year, eleventh month, tenth day), Noah let out the birds, a raven and a dove (8:6).

8. Over the next fourteen days, Noah released two more doves (8:10–12).

9. When Noah turned 601, on the first month of the first day, the waters were gone (8:13).

10. Noah waited another month and twenty-six days before he left the ark on the twenty-seventh day (8:14).

The flood took one whole year and ten days. (Read the story in Genesis 7:11–8:14.)

"I CAN HARDLY IMAGINE"

The Bible describes heaven in the following terms.

It is a place where Jesus is now building "many rooms" (John 14:1–3). Imagine the house of your dreams. Perhaps that is what Jesus is constructing right now for you.

Heaven is also a place where all of us will be spiritual, immortal, powerful, and glorious (see 1 Corinthians 15:42–44).

The book of Revelation declares the curse will be ended. No more weeds, sweat, pain, work, tears, painful childbirth—and we will eat from the tree of life. That tree has twelve different kinds of fruit. Its leaves will heal the nations (see 22:1–4).

There will be no more night, and God will "wipe every tear from [our] eyes." Death will be over, and thus no mourning or crying (21:4). God will dwell in the midst of it, and we will see his face (22:4). He will write his name on our foreheads. God will literally light up heaven—the sun won't be needed; rather God will provide all the light (22:4–5).

A new Jerusalem will be suspended in the atmosphere above the earth, and we will be able to come and go at will. This will be God's capital of the universe, and it will picture his greatness and power (21:9–27).

Above all, in heaven believers will worship, serve, and reign with Jesus forever and ever.

Will we remember our old life on earth? In Isaiah 65:17, the prophet said that God will create a world where "the former things will not be remembered, nor will they come to mind." Does he mean that we won't remember our relatives, our friends, our deeds? Perhaps. But it is far more likely that we won't remember the bad things that pained us. The glory of heaven will be so great that there will be no reason to compare our lives on earth to it (see Romans 8:18).

Don't think heaven is a place where we will sit on clouds and play harps. No, heaven will be the greatest adventure of all, and it will never end!

GOD IS LIKE A STORK

Lovingkindness. This important word is found throughout the Bible, but especially in the Old Testament. The Hebrew word is *kesed*, which is translated "loyal love," "goodness," and "kindness." It's a picturesque word, but the Spirit of God in crafting the words of the Bible gave the Hebrews a special picture that would convey to them the deeper meaning of God's loyal, loving, and kind goodness to them. Here we find a connection between the root word that the Hebrews used for God's loyal love and the name of the stork. Why would the Hebrews relate the two?

Storks, among all birds, are especially tender and kind with their young. In fact, their little ones stay longer in the nest than any other bird. This is because the mother stork, nurturing and loyal, will not force her young ones out into the world against their will and not until they're ready. The Hebrews noted the tender attitude storks had toward their young and thought, "loving and kind." So they used the same root for the word that described God's goodness and kindness to them. They thought of God as tender like this bird because he led them gently in life, not like a dictator or a harsh potentate, but like a mother stork with her little ones (see Psalm 103:8; Genesis 20:13; Jonah 2:9).

HOW TO LOVE A TERRORIST

What does the Bible say about people like Osama bin Laden? About suicide bombings, death threats, and people who commit mass murder in the name of their religion?

While the United States looks at terrorists as thoroughly evil people, the Bible does say some things about how to treat such people. The primary passage is from Jesus's Sermon on the Mount, in which he talked about how to deal with enemies. The leading Jews of Jesus's day had twisted Moses's law, which called for justice and fairness in dealing with any criminal. They believed, following the second Great Commandment—"love your neighbor as yourself"—that you should "love your neighbor and hate your enemy." They added "hate your enemy" to the biblical command; it was not in Moses's original statement. Jesus refused to approve of that addition, when he said in Matthew 5:43–48,

> You have heard that it was said, "Love your neighbor and hate your enemy." But I tell you: Love your enemies and pray for those who persecute you, that you may be sons of your Father in heaven. He causes his sun to rise on the evil

and the good, and sends rain on the righteous and the unrighteous. If you love those who love you, what reward will you get? Are not even the tax collectors doing that? And if you greet only your brothers, what are you doing more than others? Do not even pagans do that? Be perfect, therefore, as your heavenly Father is perfect.

Although it might seem strange for the Bible to command us to love and pray for our enemies, that is exactly what Jesus said. However, he was talking about the individual's attitude toward an enemy, not the government's or a nation's attitude. We are called simply to love and pray for our enemies, whoever they may be.

On the other hand, governments must uphold the law, deal justly with criminals, and punish those who offend. Paul wrote in Romans 13:1–4,

Everyone must submit himself to the governing authorities, for there is no authority except that which God has established. The authorities that exist have been established by God. Consequently, he who rebels against the authority is rebelling against what God has instituted, and those who do so will bring judgment on themselves. For rulers hold no terror for those who do right, but for those who do wrong. Do you want to be free from fear of the one in authority? Then do what is right and he will commend you. For he is God's servant to do you good. But if you do wrong, be afraid, for he does not bear the sword for nothing. He is God's servant, an agent of wrath to bring punishment on the wrongdoer.

From these verses we conclude:

1. God has established the authority to maintain the law.

2. People who rebel against the government will bring the government's judgment upon them.

3. Governments don't punish people for doing right, but for doing wrong.

4. God specifically gives the power of life and death to governments so they can deal effectively with wrongdoers.

What are we as Bible believers to do about terrorists? Pray for them. Cry out to God for their conversion to a true belief in God's justice. In whatever way we can, we are even to love them and hope for their best in this world.

But on the other hand, we are to support our government in its quest to ferret out evildoers and stop the mass murders in our world. God gave the right to carry out justice and retribution to the government, not to us as individuals. He tells us over and over to leave revenge to him. Certainly, we should follow the government's lead when they mete out justice for public wrongs, but in the end, all final revenge and justice remains in God's hands, not ours (see Romans 12:19–21).

ONE HOT LAKE

Scripture speaks of hell frequently, though not in as amazing terms as heaven.

What will it be like? Jesus said that it's a place of "weeping and gnashing of teeth" and where the soul never dies and "the fire never goes out" (Matthew 8:12; Mark 9:47–48). Revelation 20:14 tells us that hell is a "lake of fire" that never flames out. John called it "the second death" (Revelation 2:11, 20:6).

There, all evildoers will be confined so they cannot harm anyone—even their fellow prisoners—again. Every person will possess a physical body that can feel thirst, hunger, sexual desire, and pain, but they will not have any way to satisfy those desires. It will be a place of utter darkness (Jude 13), absolutely impenetrable. The lake is called "unquenchable fire" (Mark 9:43 NASB), a place of burning and "fire and brimstone" (Revelation 21:8 NASB). Hell is also "eternal punishment" (Matthew 25:46), "everlasting chains" (Jude 6), the "Abyss" (Revelation 9:2, 11), "outer darkness" (Matthew 8:12 NASB), "everlasting destruction" (2 Thessalonians 1:9).

Obviously, it's not a pleasant place. Only those who have hated God and rejected him and his Son completely will reside there. Those thrown into the "pit" will never see, hear, learn of, or taste anything from God's creation again.

If you read these words, though, and cringe, please know that faith in Christ ensures complete escape from the horrors of hell. If you find yourself worried about such a fate, simply read the Scriptures and put your faith in Christ. The Bible says, "Everyone who calls on the name of the Lord will be saved" (Romans 10:13).

IN THE NAME OF THE FATHER[20]

The Greek word for baptism is *bapto*. It means "to dip" as into water. Many scholars thus believe that baptism as done by John the Baptist and Jesus's disciples as well as the early church was a "dipping" or immersion into a pool or river of water. According to Matthew 3:6 (NASB), many people in the district around the Jordan "were being baptized by him [John the Baptist] in the Jordan River, as they confessed their sins." It would seem that if they were being baptized—i.e., "dipped"—into the Jordan River, they must have been immersed, plunged in and entirely covered in the water.

Making your way further through Matthew, you find that when Jesus was baptized, "After being baptized, Jesus came up immediately from the water" (Matthew 3:16 NASB). Again, it appears straightforward. How could Jesus "come up" from the water if he wasn't "in" it?

Other scholars argue that the same word that means "dipped" also in certain places means "washed" or "cleansed," especially in Old Testament usage. These scholars, of course, prefer sprinkling as the mode of baptism, and this is the most prevalent mode you find in the Christian church today—Roman Catholics, Presbyterians, Episcopalians, Congregationalists, and many others practice sprinkling instead of immersion.

Regardless of the kind of baptism one undergoes, the primary point is what it signifies. John the Baptist preached a "baptism of repentance." It represented cleansing—internally, spiritually, emotionally.

Jesus took it further, identifying baptism as a picture of being "born again" (see John 3). Baptism outwardly demonstrates the internal transformation. It also shows inclusion in the body of Christ. By baptism we are spiritually "dipped" into the body of Christ, immersed and at one with Jesus forever.

Paul the apostle further augmented the idea. In Romans 6:3–5 Paul wrote that baptism—being dipped into the water and coming up again—represented our identification with Christ in his death and resurrection. Thus, when we are baptized, we are buried with Christ in his death and raised again to new life through his resurrection.

All the forms of baptism used in the church today—immersion, sprinkling, and effusion (pouring water out of a cup onto your head)—represent elements of this single act. Immersion shows our death with Christ and our rising again with him to new life. Sprinkling shows the cleansing and the act of being "dyed" or "changed" so that we are new people in Christ. Effusion pictures the "pouring out" of the Holy Spirit upon the new believer so that he is animated and filled with divine power. These ordinances are all based on strong and long-held traditions in the various churches that employ them. Whatever mode of baptism you choose does not seem to be the Bible's or God's concern. Rather, it's the fact that you have been changed through repentance and faith that matters; baptism simply represents your new stance and commitment to Christ, to the church, and to God's people.

The only other question that remains is who should be baptized? Some traditions believe only those who have reached an age where they can understand what they're doing should be baptized. This means children under the age of four or five probably should not be baptized. Some churches use an "age of accountability," a time in life when each person can make an informed and solemn decision about his or her relationship to Christ. Many consider the age of accountability to be around ten to thirteen years old, when a juvenile can make a realistic and honest decision about Christ. These kinds of churches practice "believer's baptism." Only those who have exercised real faith in Christ can be baptized.

The predominant tradition you find in the church today is "infant baptism." Usually the infant is sprinkled with water, representing his or her inclusion in the covenant as the son or daughter of believers. This tradition is based on the early teaching of the church under St. Augustine and others who held that baptism in the New Testament was similar to circumcision in the Old Testament. Circumcision was performed on Jewish boys at the age of eight days, and it signified inclusion, protection, and all the rights and privileges of being under God's rule and love. Infant baptism pictured the same idea. A newborn required the protection and power of God's care. His parents believed, and baptism showed their commitment to transmitting their faith to the child and the whole church's desire to raise him or her in the covenant faith.

Many Christians today argue vociferously about the mode, meaning, and participants in baptism. Baptists believe one thing. Roman Catholics another. And Presbyterians still another. Each of these traditions is based on ardent and committed study of the Scriptures. Considering the divisiveness that baptism has caused in the church over the years, it seems wise that each person should be convinced in his own mind. That is, we are each required to study, meditate on, and reach our own conclusions—and then practice them in faith during our sojourn on this earth. One day in heaven we'll all know the exact truth. But until then, we are called to love one another as Christ has loved us—despite our differences and opinions.

HOW TO COME TO KNOW THE GOD OF THE BIBLE

Here is a simple statement of how to start a relationship with God through Jesus Christ.

1. Consider what you've read about Jesus, God, the Bible, and so on, and decide whether you believe it (Acts 16:31).

2. Examine your life in light of the Bible and admit you have broken God's laws and rules (Romans 3:23).

3. Decide whether you believe Jesus is God incarnate and can forgive your sins, make you a new person on the inside, and lead you to live in a God-honoring way (Acts 4:9–10; John 1:12).

4. Call on God in Christ and ask him to open your eyes to the truth, come into your life, and begin transforming you into the kind of person he wants you to be (Romans 10:13).

5. Tell someone who is a Christian that you have accepted Christ. Go to a church where God's Word is believed and taught, and apply yourself to follow Christ all the days of your life (Romans 10:9–10).

If you have taken these steps, then I welcome you to the kingdom of God. Your life, I guarantee, will begin to change in amazing ways in the days ahead. Talk to God as much as you can, read his Word and study it, memorize passages that speak to you in a special way, go to church and start to get involved, and tell others about what has happened to you. Expect God to make himself real to you (see John 14:23). Pray about everything important to you, no matter how trivial it may seem, and expect God to answer in ways you can never expect. Above all, don't give up, even when bad things happen to you. God will be using everything in your life, even the bad stuff, to bring about good (see Romans 8:28). So expect to see him every day in some situation, circumstance, person, or answer to prayer. He has plans for your life, so trust him to lead you (see Jeremiah 29:11–13). Every day, opportunities to do good will come your way. God has put these events into your life for a purpose (see Ephesians 2:10), so expect many incredible things to happen in the days ahead.

Thanks for reading. I hope this book has enlightened you in a multitude of ways. I'm very excited that you've stuck with me to the end. And if I don't meet you in this world, I'm quite sure we'll meet in the next.

Until then, Maranatha, which means, "Our Lord, come."

NOTES

1. Josh McDowell, *Evidence that Demands a Verdict* (Nashville: Nelson, 1999), 63.
2. Adapted from H. L. Willmington, *Willmington's Book of Bible Lists* (Wheaton, Ill.: Tyndale House, 1987), 183–86.
3. McDowell, 66–68
4. Willmington, 122–23.
5. David Wallechinsky and Irving Wallace, *The People's Almanac* (Garden City, NY: Doubleday, 1975), 1286–87.
6. Adapted from "Bible," www.wikipedia.com.
7. Charles Colson, *Loving God* (Grand Rapids, Mich.: Zondervan, 1983), 55.
8. Adapted from *Decision* magazine, July, 1978.
9. Adapted from Willmington, 119.
10. Adapted from Willmington, 260–63.
11. Adapted from McDowell.

12. Adapted from G. Y. Craig, and E. J. Jones, *A Geological Miscellany* (Princeton University Press, 1982).

13. Adapted from Mark Littleton, *Jesus: Everything You Need to Know to Figure Him Out* (Louisville, Ky.: Westminster, 2001).

14. Adapted from Mark Littleton, *The Books of the Bible: All Your Questions Answered* (Cabot, Ark.: Halo Press, 1995).

15. Adapted from Littleton, *Book of the Bible.*

16. Adapted from Littleton, *Book of the Bible.*

17. Merrill C. Tenney, ed., *Pictorial Bible Dictionary* (Grand Rapids, Mich.: Zondervan, 1967), 281.

18. Wallechinsky and Wallace, 1286–87.

19. Adapted from Littleton, *Jesus.*

20. Adapted from Littleton, *Book of the Bible.*